Servant of the Crown

A Civil Servant's Story of Criminal Justice
and Public Service Reform

David Faulkner

With a Foreword by Sir John Chilcot

☵ WATERSIDE PRESS

Servant of the Crown
A Civil Servant's Story of Criminal Justice and Public Service Reform

ISBN 978-1-909976-02-3 (Paperback)
ISBN 978-1-908162-75-5 (Epub ebook)
ISBN 978-1-908162-76-2 (Adobe ebook)

Cover design © 2014 Waterside Press. Design by www.gibgob.com.

Main UK distributor Gardners Books, 1 Whittle Drive, Eastbourne, East Sussex, BN23 6QH. Tel: +44 (0)1323 521777; sales@gardners.com; www.gardners.com

North American distribution Ingram Book Company, One Ingram Blvd, La Vergne, TN 37086, USA. Tel: (+1) 615 793 5000; inquiry@ingramcontent.com

Cataloguing-In-Publication Data A catalogue record for this book can be obtained from the British Library.

Printed by CPI Group, Chippenham, UK.

e-book *Servant of the Crown* is available as an ebook and also to subscribers of Myilibrary, Dawsonera, ebrary, and Ebscohost.

Published 2014 by
Waterside Press
Sherfield Gables
Sherfield-on-Loddon
Hook, Hampshire
United Kingdom RG27 0JG

Telephone +44(0)1256 882250
E-mail enquiries@watersidepress.co.uk
Online catalogue WatersidePress.co.uk

Contents

David Faulkner reflects on his long and distinguished career in the Civil Service to raise crucial questions not only about criminal justice but also about government, about state and citizen and the proper roles of civil servants and politicians. His insistence on the priority of trying to do the right thing gives a prominence to ethics that is sadly lacking in so much current criminal justice debate.

Rob Canton, Professor in Community and Criminal
Justice, De Montford University

Throughout a remarkable career in public service at the Home Office, David Faulkner played an invaluable role in the making of criminal justice policy. His book enriches our understanding of its history, character and development over the past half century.

David Downes, Professor Emiritus of Social Administration at
the London School of Economics and Political Science

This is a book about the changing relationship between senior civil servants, government and ultimately citizens. David Faulkner gives an erudite personal history of his time at the Home Office with wisdom and a sense of humanity and humility. He eloquently argues for a rethinking of the values underpinning public service beyond the managerialist malaise of the day. This volume is both timely and timeless in its relevance and will be read by scholars and students of today and in the future. Anyone interested in the state and its relationship to citizens should read it, I very warmly welcome its arrival.

Graham Towl, Professor in the Department of Psychology, Pro-
Vice Chancellor and Deputy Warden, Durham University

Acknowledgements

I felt some hesitation about embarking on a more personal story than I had written before, concerned that it might seem self-regarding or nostalgic, but several friends and former colleagues persuaded me that I had something useful to say and encouraged me to make the attempt.

I would particularly like to thank Andrew Ashworth, Ros Burnett, Bill Burnham, Rob Canton, David Downes, Richard Faulkner, Tim Flesher, Cedric Fullwood, Ann James, Joanna Kozubska, Lisa Miller, Michael Moriarty, Graham Towl, Michael Wheeler-Booth and Philip Whitehead, both for encouraging me to think that the enterprise was worthwhile in the first place, and then for their supportive comments on the draft chapters which they have been kind enough to read. The book would not have written without their encouragement and it would have suffered without their suggestions and corrections, but any opinions I have expressed and any mistakes I have made are my own.

I would also like to pay tribute to the many friends, colleagues and contacts with whom I have worked over what is now a period of 55 years from my arrival in the Home Office to the present. From them I learned what I knew of the techniques, skills and values of public administration and public service, both in the Home Office and in the wider fields of criminal justice and public service, and later the insights and perspectives which came from academic analysis and discussion and from work with the voluntary sector. They include the trustees of the Thames Valley Partnership, and the group of (now mostly retired) public servants who periodically meet in and around Thame in Oxfordshire. They are too numerous to be acknowledged individually, but many of their names appear in the chapters which follow. I would like this book to be a tribute to their effort and integrity, and to the inspiration which I gained from them. It has, as always, been a great pleasure to work with Bryan Gibson at Waterside Press.

David Faulkner
June 2014

About the Author

David Faulkner is well-known for his acclaimed works *Crime State and Citizen* (2006) and *Where Next for Criminal Justice?* (with Ross Burnett) (2012). Before teaching and researching at Oxford University he spent his working life in the Civil Service, including at the Home Office (dealing with certain areas now the responsibility of the Ministry of Justice) and in the Cabinet Office. He was appointed CB in 1985.

Articles by the author relevant to this book also appear at the Waterside Press website: www.WatersidePress.co.uk.

Foreword

By the Rt Hon Sir John Chilcot, GCB

This is a uniquely rewarding book on several levels. It contains a narrative through several decades of the key issues and developments in the field of criminal justice and penal policy, from the standpoint of one of the most influential senior civil servants working in that field. It is also a riveting account of the personal and intellectual formation of someone who, as all who knew and worked with him, was at once profoundly and conscientiously serious, and deeply engaged with the underlying human troubles with which public policy on crime and punishment has continually to struggle.

More than that, it illustrates the tensions, unavoidable and capable of being either fruitful or destructive, and sometimes both, between political realities and aspirational policy-making. That is sometimes portrayed, simplistically, as a battle between elected and accountable politicians in office, together these days with their political advisers on the one hand and on the other the permanent civil servants. David Faulkner's insightful story shows how limited such a polarised view is, with his own engagement over many years not only with politicians in (and sometimes out of) office, but also with academia, opinion formers and interest groups of many varieties, the media in its Protean variety, the third sector, and most important of all, the practitioners—judges and magistrates, lawyers, prison and probation staff and many others.

One theme that runs through this piece of recent and contemporary policy history is the combination of ever more pressing resource constraints with the mounting recognition that the unpredictable ebbs and flows of human behaviour (and misbehaviour) make rational evidence-based policy-making a hazardous enterprise at best. Even the most imaginative or securely evidenced policy initiatives face a bright beam of scrutiny which often illuminates flaws and defects in practice. You have to have, as the author exemplifies, not only great resilience and determination, but an acceptance of both self-examination and critical, sometimes hostile, reactions from others. There is no trace here of a tired settling back into passive acquiescence in the way things are, or are being shifted by events, or shallow thinking.

Two other things about this book struck this reader. The first is the colour and life which often shines through. A case in point is the author's generous tribute to James Callaghan's initiative in Northern Ireland at the end of the sixties (which I too applaud for its political courage, though it was too late as events turned out after all the years of political neglect by Westminster). As Callaghan's Principal Private Secretary, David Faulkner had a famously difficult working relationship with Callaghan, at a time when the latter's political fortunes were strained, to put it mildly, so the author's generosity is the more notable.

The other is the marked continuity of the cast of characters engaged in criminal justice and penal policy from the sixties to the nineties. This had, in the face of all the shifts of circumstance, opinion and even intellectual fashion over the period, a positive impact by conserving understanding and intellectual capital in the field. Without it, public policy-making would have been even more variable than it has been. David Faulkner's contribution is a powerful summation of that virtue so much admired by Montaigne, where strong opinions are held in balance by moderation, and accepting the limits of the feasible without losing the drive to make things better.

Introduction

This book draws together some of my experiences and recollections of criminal justice and of the Home Office where I was a civil servant from 1959 until 1992, with later reflections from my time as an associate at the University of Oxford Centre for Criminological Research, later the Centre for Criminology and as a fellow of St John's College Oxford until 1999. The book's focus is partly on crime and criminal justice, the changes that took place and the factors that prompted or constrained them; but it also includes some personal impressions of the Home Office itself as a department of state, the interaction between ministers and officials, its relations with the judiciary and the public services for which it had responsibility, and the civil servant's role as a 'servant of the Crown'. Most of the functions with which I was concerned are the responsibility of the Ministry of Justice, formed in 2007.

Crime and Responses to Crime

The story of crime and the response to crime in England and Wales over the last 60 years is part of the larger story of the social and political changes which have taken place during that time. For most of the third quarter of the 20th-century the debate was moving in a broadly 'liberal' direction — the abolition of capital and judicial corporal punishment, improved conditions in prisons, better support for offenders after release, greater safeguards against injustice. The last quarter brought changes in the patterns and expectations of employment and of social and family life, in the character and composition of communities, and in attitudes to authority. Some fears, for example of disease, diminished or disappeared; others, including the fear of crime, took their place. Society became more individualistic, placing greater emphasis on personal achievement, failure and responsibility, while old certainties and loyalties — to institutions, political parties, religious faiths or communities — have been weakened or lost.

The period saw first a rise and then, after the mid-1990s, a fall in the volume of reported and surveyed crime. The reasons are complicated and they are still in dispute. Short-lived confidence in the ability of the criminal justice system to 'solve' the problem of crime through a combination of scientific policing and the sophisticated assessment and treatment of offenders gave way to disillusion and scepticism, and then to a tentative but later more confident belief in 'what works' to reduce re-offending. Governments, services and interest groups became increasingly aware of the needs and expectations of victims; the significance of ethnicity, race and gender; and the scope for reducing crime through physical, situational and social measures that do not involve the criminal justice process.

Public and political attitudes became less tolerant of crime and more punitive towards those who commit it. As criminal justice gained a higher political salience, ministers became more ready to intervene and the services, like others in the public sector, became more centrally managed and directed according to political priorities. In prisons the emphasis moved at various times from treatment and conditions to security and control and back again. Probation was transformed from a social work agency serving its clients to a publicly accountable criminal justice service serving the courts and then to an agency of law enforcement and public protection.

For the last 20 years, the movement has mostly been away from the 'liberal consensus' and a new political consensus has been built around greater certainty of conviction, more severe sentencing and more punitive treatment of those convicted. The courts' discretion in sentencing has been progressively constrained by legislation and guidelines, at first to limit the use of imprisonment and promote sentences served in the community but then to require more and longer prison sentences to be imposed for certain offences and in certain circumstances. Social science research had at first a significant but then declining influence on policy and practice. The prison population in England and Wales rose from about 28,000 to over 85,000 in 2014 the most rapid increases taking place in the 1960s and then from 1993 onwards.

The Home Office itself was transformed, briefly gaining responsibility for broadcasting during the 1970s and early-1980s but mostly losing responsibilities to other departments—children, Northern Ireland, magistrates' courts, the Fire Service—and the Home Office that remained was then divided when the Ministry of Justice was formed in 2007. Traditional sources of advice such as commissions, committees and civil servants themselves gave way to consultants and politically aligned think-tanks. Loss of continuity and changes in patterns of careers and career development weakened the department's sense of identity and collective memory and what might be called its departmental wisdom. Those features themselves became less valued as more issues became matters of political rather than departmental or professional judgement, and came to be seen less as strengths and more as obstacles to progress. The present Coalition government has an ideological belief in the capacity of the private sector to achieve a transformation through a process of commissioning and payment by results.

What this Book is About

The book complements my earlier accounts in *Crime State and Citizen* and *Where Next for Criminal Justice?*,[1] the latter written with Ros Burnett, but it is more selective in concentrating on those issues and events with which I was personally concerned and my impressions of them. Lord Windlesham has given a more comprehensive account of some of those events in his *Responses to Crime*, especially in Volume 2,[2] and Andrew Rutherford has described my own approach to them in Chapter 5 of *Transforming Criminal Policy*.[3] Ian Loader has examined the 'governance of crime' and the decline in the influence of civil servants like myself in his article 'Fall of the Platonic Guardians'.[4] Other accounts include Ian Dunbar's and Anthony Langdon's *Tough Justice*,[5] Mick Ryan's *Penal Policy and Political Culture*,[6] and from a broader perspective David Garland's *Culture of Control*.[7] My objective in this book is not to repeat what has been said elsewhere, but to give a more personal account of the events with which I was most involved and of what

1. David Faulkner *Crime, State and Citizen: A Field Full of Folk,* Sherfield-on-Loddon: Waterside Press, second edition 2006; David Faulkner and Ros Burnett *Where Next for Criminal Justice?*, Bristol: The Policy Press, 2011.

2. Lord Windlesham, *Responses to Crime,* Vol 2, *Penal Policy in the Making,* Oxford: Clarendon Press, 1993.

3. Andrew Rutherford *Transforming Criminal Policy*, Sherfield-on-Loddon: Waterside Press, 1996.

4. Ian Loader 'Fall of the Platonic Guardians: Liberalism, Criminology and Political Responses to Crime in England and Wales', *British Journal of Criminology* (2006), 46, 561-586.

5. Ian Dunbar and Anthony Langdon *Tough Justice: Sentencing and Penal Policies in the 1990s,* London: Blackstone, 1998.

6. Mick Ryan *Penal Policy and Political Culture in England and Wales*, Sherfield-on-Loddon: Waterside Press, 2003.

7. David Garland *The Culture of Control: Crime and Social Order in Contemporary Society,* Oxford: Oxford University Press, 2001.

I thought and felt about them; and to describe my own perception of the attitudes, beliefs and values which lay behind them.

In the chapters which follow I explain my own involvement in those processes and describe what I did or tried to do and what I thought, both at the time and subsequently in retrospect and from a different perspective. In *Chapter 1* I describe my impressions of the Home Office as I found it at the end of the 1950s. *Chapters 2* and *3* describe how I saw prisons and the Prison Department at different periods of time — the mid-1960s, the early-1970s and the early-1980s. *Chapters 5* to *9* describe the government's policies towards crime and criminal justice during the 1980s, their context, and how they were formulated. *Chapter 10* is about the Home Office during the period but especially as it was at the beginning of the 1990s, and *Chapter 11* brings together some later reflections on themes drawn from my time in the Home Office as a whole. *Chapter 12* describes the work I have done since I left the Home Office and the present situation as I see it, and offers some conclusions.

The book is not intended to be a collection of memoirs or a personal life history, but rather a commentary on criminal justice and the Home Office and a story about them. I have not said much about those periods in my time at the Home Office which were not part of that story — civil defence, House of Lords reform, and the Cabinet Office — although (from the last two especially) I learned a lot about the working of the party political machines and the tension between the national interest (however that is defined) and party political advantage. I describe how the Home Office behaved as a department; the relationship between ministers and officials as I experienced it; how the department set about decision-making and the formation and implementation of policy; and how I tried to do my job — the ways of doing things that seemed to work or not work at the time, and which might work for other people in other situations.

I have also tried to illustrate the values and culture which I see as implicit in the criminal justice process in this country, and which informed the approaches which successive governments' policies took towards it. I hope the story will be of historical interest to scholars and practitioners, and perhaps to those who have similar responsibilities today; and that it may also have some relevance to the continuing debate both about criminal justice and about Civil Service reform.

I was only one among many colleagues involved in the events I have described, in the Home Office, other government departments and the relevant services and occupations. They all made their own contributions and will have their own recollections, impressions and opinions which may not be the same as my own. I do not claim to speak for them in any way, and there may be times when my memory is at fault, but I owed a great deal to them and I was and still am grateful for their inspiration, guidance and support.

It is not a story of high drama, new revelations or biting criticisms, but of people trying conscientiously to do our jobs in circumstances of complexity, uncertainty and compromise; to make things better where we could; and to do so with some sense of purpose in which we could believe.

CHAPTER 1

Confidence and Optimism

The Home Office as I Found It

The Home Office at the end of the 1950s was a confident place. Ministers and officials were conscious that it was one of the 'great departments of state', with a Secretary of State as its ministerial head at a time before the title came to be applied generally to members of the Cabinet. We used the titles Permanent, Deputy and Assistant Under-Secretary of State for the three most senior Civil Service grades. The heart of the Home Office was still the old main building opposite the Cenotaph in Whitehall, with its large rooms and high ceilings, its 'quadrangle' of wide corridors and its open coal fires in winter, although the less prestigious offices in the attics and the basement were very different and much of the work was done in less grand buildings in Holborn and Horseferry Road.[1] The department still had its more obscure responsibilities for subjects such as dangerous dogs, gambling, safety in the home, liquor licensing and the Carlisle and District State Management Scheme with its public houses, hotels and brewery. It sometimes described itself as the 'channel of communication between the Crown and its subjects': we did not often pause to wonder what that might mean in practice, but in later years I liked to think of the Home Office as the guardian of the relationship between the state and the citizen.

There was a sense that the department's responsibilities for justice and the constitution and its relationship with the Crown set it a bit apart from other departments. Such an elitist view could not have been expressed aloud in the Home Office from the 1960s onwards, but other departments still sometimes thought us arrogant, stuffy and presumptuous. Some Home Secretaries seemed themselves to feel that there was something special about the office they held, and that they had to be more than politicians—a sense

---

1. The only passenger lift had no level access from the front entrance and was set to run slowly in case, so it was said, the Queen Mother ever wanted to use it on Remembrance Sunday. She never did.

which James Callaghan and William Whitelaw expressed at the bicentenary lectures in 1982 described in *Chapter 5*.

Departmental Culture and Values

The Home Office saw its main functions as being to 'maintain the Queen's Peace' (understood as covering crime as well as public order); to preserve 'freedom under the law'; and to protect the 'liberty of the subject'. In a talk to staff a few months before I joined, the Permanent Secretary, Sir Charles Cunningham (from 1957 to 1966) had spoken of the Home Office as having a 'living tradition ... of the need to see that the Queen's Peace is kept, that justice is done between one citizen and another; above all, that human rights and individual freedom are not impaired'. A principle which my first boss and mentor Wilfred Hyde impressed on me during my earliest weeks in the department was that people should generally be allowed to do what they wanted to do, and if the state wanted to stop them it had to justify its action in doing so. Another was that powers granted by Parliament for one purpose should not be used for another. A principle jealously guarded by the Criminal Department was that criminal offences should only be created if the behaviour to be criminalised could not be dealt with by other means; penalties should be proportionate to the harm done and consistent with those for other offences of similar seriousness; and there should be appropriate defences and safeguards against oppressive enforcement. Punishment was a matter for the courts; people were sent to prison as punishment and not for punishment, and prison regimes and probation programmes were not to be made deliberately unpleasant for their punitive effect (although not all prison officers might agree).

The Rule of Law and the independence of the judiciary were accepted without question. Human rights were assumed to be already fully protected by existing statutes and the common law, including those set out in the European Convention on Human Rights. We were 'servants of the Crown' and were surrounded by its symbols without having much occasion to wonder what that meant. We were schooled in the doctrine that as officials we had no identity of our own and always acted in the person of the minister, but the weakness of its implication that the minister had to take personal responsibility for everything we did was already becoming apparent (see *Chapter*

11). Charles Cunningham told me on my first day of Herbert Morrison's[2] description of its corridors as being 'paved with dynamite'.

The Home Office was still recognisably the same as it was in Sir Harold Scott's description of the department as it had been in the 1920s and 1930s,[3] but it was less complacent and it became much less complacent in the years that followed. The early and mid-1960s are often thought of as a period of liberal reform, and so they were in many ways, but we did not think of ourselves as driving that process in any visionary way so much as doing what we could to make things better—more efficient, more fair, more suited to what was expected. We were more often criticised for lack of humanity than for being soft on crime. We were conscious of the more punitive views that were also being expressed in newspapers and elsewhere, but we did not feel that we had to be on the defensive against them, and I think the same was true of ministers.

The process of policy making, across government as a whole but perhaps especially in criminal justice and education, was still to a large extent informed by reports from expert advisory bodies. They might be royal commissions or departmental committees set up to carry out a specific inquiry, or standing advisory bodies such as the Advisory Council on the Treatment of Offenders (later the Advisory Council on the Penal System) and the Criminal Law Revision Committee. They were composed of men and women who were sometimes referred to as 'the great and the good', at first with respect but then disparagingly when they came to be criticised as unelected and unrepresentative.[4] They did however have specialised knowledge and experience in their own fields, established professional reputations, and no political positions which they had to defend. Their reports may have taken some time to produce, but they were well-considered and well-respected by those who had to act upon them. Policies based on them, such as those described in *Chapters 2* and *3*, were arguably no less, and probably more, successful and had a longer life, than many of those which were adopted as a result of

---

2. Home Secretary during the Second World War.
3. Harold Scott *Your Obedient Servant*, London: Andre Deutsch, 1959.
4. For example by Mick Ryan in *Penal Policy and Political Culture*, Sherfield-on-Loddon: Waterside Press, 2003.

quicker, more politically directed reviews in later years[5].

The relationship between the Home Office and its statutory services — police, probation, and the magistrates' courts and fire services — was based on the principle that the department was responsible for the legislation and funding but it was for chief officers to manage their services and take the operational decisions. Most changes in practice — professional, managerial or operational — had their origins in the services themselves, with the understanding that they usually 'knew best'. Changes might be proposed by a Royal Commission or a departmental committee, but they would not be unilaterally imposed by Home Office ministers or officials. The principle, or perhaps it should be said the theory, of chief constables' operational independence was generally accepted — by the Home Office, Parliament, the judiciary and of course the police themselves — and it was in practice extended to the chief officers of other services. Originally understood as a matter of justice — the government should not decide how statutory powers should be used against, or for the benefit of, particular individuals — it was also understood as applying to the management of their services.[6]

Most work was done with meticulous care and attention to detail, precedent and correct procedure, sometimes but not often at great speed, and those outside the department often thought we were stuffy, slow, arbitrary, exclusive and obsessed by precedent. An important skill was to 'say "no" nicely and not too soon'. Idiosyncrasy and sometimes incompetence were tolerated on a scale which would not be accepted today and ought not to have been accepted then, although not, I thought, on a large scale. There was a strong departmental memory, reinforced by the importance which was attached to precedent and by a system of 'noting' significant decisions so that they could easily be found and referred to on future occasions. We were inclined to be reticent if ever we were with people or in situations that

5.   Such as the changes to the structure of the probation service and the creation of the National Offender Management Service in 2003. See Patrick Carter *Managing Offenders, Reducing Crime: A New Approach,* London: Prime Minister's Strategy Unit, 2003. For a commentary, see Mike Hough, Rob Allen and Una Padel (eds.) *Reshaping Prisons and Probation: the New Offender Management Framework,* Bristol: The Policy Press, 2006.
6.   See Tim Newburn 'The Accountability of Policing' in Tim Newburn (ed) *Handbook of Policing,* second edition, Cullompton: Willan, 2008.

were outside our comfort zone (where we did not venture very often), and we tried to avoid any risk of public criticism, but I do not remember that the Official Secrets Acts were themselves a serious constraint. There was little formal training and not much attempt to monitor or manage performance.

It was not a culture that encouraged innovation or risk-taking, but individuals who wanted to be adventurous would often find support. The department encouraged good practice and allowed imagination in the services for which it had responsibility; it usually worked on a basis of trust, and was not inclined to look for or suspect incompetence or abuse unless it came to notice in a way that could not be ignored. As elsewhere, issues of race or gender were not seen as serious concerns and women were generally treated with respect as colleagues although there were not many in senior positions. I would like to think that for the most part, despite some well-justified criticisms, we did our work with complete integrity and as much humanity as possible, consistently with the law, political reality and policy as it was defined. We were very clear about, and proud of, our accountability to ministers and Parliament, and Parliamentary debates, Questions and correspondence were taken very seriously indeed.

Ministers, Structure and Organization

Ministers were not such a strong presence as they later became. The ministerial team in the 1950s and 1960s consisted only of the Home Secretary and two or three junior ministers, with a much smaller private office and press office, and political advisers had not yet appeared.[7] There was very little interference from the Prime Minister's office, and No 10 Downing Street itself had only a small staff. Apart from the Public Accounts Committee, there were no effective select committees. The Cabinet Office and especially the Cabinet secretary were important and influential, but they did not have the capacity or the inclination to introduce or carry through any initiatives of their own. There was less legislation and fewer initiatives which were taken at ministers' own instigation or with which they needed or wanted to be personally associated. They were under less pressure to appear in the

---

7. Roy Jenkins appointed Anthony (later Lord) Lester and John (later Lord) Harris as special advisers in 1965 but unlike many of the political advisers appointed in later years they were experts with established reputations in their respective fields.

news or prove themselves to the public or the Prime Minister. They spent more time out of the office, in their constituencies or elsewhere.[8] Michael Moriarty has said

> It has struck me looking back that for much of the time their character was less that of a full-time executive director, and the main source of initiatives in policy and administration, that seems more recently to have developed. Many had, or had until appointment, substantial extra-Parliamentary interests and even part time careers. They had to attend to their [House of Commons] lives and their constituencies, all with minimal support…[9]

The change towards greater activity and involvement began with Roy Jenkins' appointment as Home Secretary in 1965, and it rapidly gathered momentum after Margaret Thatcher became Prime Minister in 1979.

Most people in the Home Office had been there for all their working lives and expected to stay until they retired, although a period in another department, including the Cabinet Office or the Prime Minister's Office, was useful for those who hoped to reach the highest positions. Within the Home Office people moved quite often between different parts of the department, commonly at intervals of three to five years and without much choice about where they were sent. The basic unit of management was the 'division', headed by an assistant secretary (now grade 5). Three or four divisions would form a 'department' headed by an assistant under-secretary of state (now a director), and three or four departments reported to a deputy under-secretary of state (now a director general). Divisions were known by a combination of letters and numbers (C1, P4): the letters sometimes indicated the department's area of responsibility (C—Criminal, P—Prisons), but not always (B—Immigration and F—Police). The arrangement had an historical explanation and was well understood by insiders, but it was incomprehensible to anyone else.

All work was supposed to be done, and all decisions were supposed to be

---

8.   R A Butler spent much of the summer on the Island of Mull, with ministerial boxes travelling by train to Oban and then on a small boat. Telephone calls were routed through the local manual exchange situated in the village shop.

9.   In personal correspondence.

taken, 'on the file'. The file contained all the current and previous papers relevant to the subject, or 'case' if it was about an individual. Files would travel
between desks, 'horizontally' if another part of the department was being
consulted or 'upwards' if it was being submitted to more senior officials or
to ministers for approval or action. Files had two 'sides'. The right hand side
was for substantive papers — correspondence, submissions,[10] circulated or
published documents and drafts; the left hand side was for 'minutes' giving
comments or explanations or making proposals, with occasional flashes of
humour. A file might grow until it had several 'sub-numbers' containing older
papers (a notorious long-serving prisoner might in time generate over 100),
and the whole file was supposed to travel together with the sub-numbers tied
together by white tape. Other files might be attached if they were relevant,
and the whole bundle was tied together by blue tape. Red or yellow flags
would be attached if the matter was 'immediate' or 'pressing', or a pink flag
if it was a 'minister's case' (for example a reply to a letter from a Member of
Parliament). The system must now seem very quaint, but it did ensure that
there was a complete and accessible record of the actions and decisions that
were taken and the reasons for them.

Unless a senior officer's personal secretary could be persuaded to help,
all typing for grades below the rank of assistant secretary had to be sent to
a typing pool, often outside London, and might take a week or ten days
to come back. Photocopiers were not yet in use, and if more than carbon
copies were needed it was necessary to cut a stencil and roll the copies off
on the machine a page at a time.

The department was (as it would now seem) unbelievably centralised. Sir
Charles Cunningham insisted that all submissions to the Home Secretary
should go forward over his own signature. Most correspondence with
members of the public, for example replies to applications, complaints or
requests for information, was rigidly (and it might now be thought comically)
formal — 'I am directed by the Secretary of State … I am, Sir (or Madam),
your obedient servant'. That form of address and the style of writing that
went with it were for a long time defended as necessary to comply with the
constitutional doctrine. It would be a fair criticism to say that too much
attention was sometimes paid to drafting, with successive amendments being

---

10. Papers making proposals to ministers.

made as a draft passed 'up the chain', but we did pay attention to Sir Ernest Gowers' advice in *Plain Words*[11] and tried to avoid the kind of jargon that became prevalent in later years.

Younger members of staff used first names among themselves but for older male colleagues last names alone were still the rule. Women were addressed as 'Miss' or 'Mrs' and they addressed their male colleagues as 'Mr'. 'Sir' was used by messengers and doorkeepers or when speaking to royalty, but not otherwise. It would have been unthinkable for a civil servant to address the Home Secretary or a minister except as 'Home Secretary' or 'Minister'.

Issues at the Time

People were always conscious that an explosive issue could blow up at any time, and I soon learned that nothing in the Home Office is ever simple. But what came to be called the criminal justice system seemed to be working reasonably well, with no immediate need for legislation (the last Criminal Justice Act had been in 1948), or administrative reform (apart from the integration of the Prison Commission into the main Home Office, see *Chapter 2*). In criminal justice the main political issue was capital punishment, the end of which for most people in the Home Office could not come too soon. Prison overcrowding was beginning to be an issue, but the borstal system (see *Chapter 3*) was still seen as the jewel in the crown of the Prison Service and Sir Lionel Fox, the chairman of the Prison Commission, still presented it as an example to the world. The more scientific methods in the treatment of offenders set out in the white paper *Penal Practice in a Changing Society*[12] were thought to provide a solution to the problems of criminality and reoffending, and similar optimism was repeated in the subsequent white paper *The War Against Crime in England and Wales*[13] (despite what I would now see as its unfortunate use of the word 'war' in its title). The period has sometimes been portrayed as one of political consensus which came to an end in the campaign for the 1979 election, but my impression was not so much that there was a consensus between the political parties but that criminal justice,

---

11.   Sir Ernest Gowers *The Complete Plain Words*, London: HMSO, 1958
12.   Home Office *Penal Practice in a Changing Society*, Cmnd 645, London: HMSO, 1959.
13.   Home Office *The War against Crime in England and Wales, 1959-1963*, Cmnd 2296. London: HMSO, 1964.

apart from capital punishment, had a lower political profile and there was a less confrontational style of politics more generally.

With support from R A Butler as Home Secretary, Sir Charles Cunningham as Permanent Secretary and senior officials such as Francis Graham-Harrison, the Home Office Research Unit under Tom Lodge grew in size and influence, alongside the Cambridge Institute of Criminology with its director Leon Radzinowicz and the centres that were becoming established in Oxford and the London School of Economics. Both in the Home Office and in Parliament, with encouragement from supporters such as Hugh Klare, the secretary of the Howard League for Penal Reform, there was more interest in understanding criminal behaviour and in improving the help and support available to offenders and ex-offenders, than in devising more severe forms of punishment, or it has to be said in providing recognition and help for victims of crime.

Elsewhere in the department, defence against the possibility of a nuclear attack was still a major preoccupation and took a large share of the department's administrative resources. In immigration the main concern was still the need to prevent the admission of economic migrants for settlement or potential spies or subversives from Communist countries. The British Nationality Act 1948, giving British nationality and a right of entry to the citizens the old British Empire, seemed to be working well, and the need to control immigration from the Commonwealth was only just beginning to appear on the horizon. Then as now, extradition (removal to another country at that country's instigation) and deportation (removal on the order of the secretary of state) were the most potentially explosive subjects. The Home Office still had responsibility for children and exercised its oversight of local authority children's departments through its well-regarded children's inspectorate. There were periodical scandals in approved schools, but their existence as institutions was not yet seriously challenged.

CHAPTER 2

Prisons and Politics — the 1960s

My first postings were to the Aliens Department (as it then was) and then to the division which had responsibility for approving byelaws and advising Parliament on private bills. Those were followed by a period as private secretary to Charles Fletcher-Cooke, the Parliamentary under-Secretary of State. I had no formal training apart from a basic three-week 'Treasury course' on management.

Early in 1963 I was seconded to the Prison Commission, which became the Prison Department of the Home Office when the commission was dissolved later in the year. The change had been discussed for many years. Its opponents, who included most of the Prison Service apart from its most senior members, feared that the Home Office would be remote and out of touch and that its dead hand would suppress the energy and imagination which was to be found in the Prison Service. Later commentators such as Lord Windlesham[1] have seen it as a mistake. In reality, the nominal independence of the commission had by then become a source of frustration, not least for the commission itself. The statutory distinction between the powers of the Secretary of State and those of the commission led to constant cross-referencing, duplication, and sometimes indecision and misunderstanding. The commissioners became the Prisons Board, with the same composition and in many respects the same functions, but they were now able to exercise the full statutory powers of the Secretary of State, and the new board and Prison Department as a whole had more independence and effective powers than the Prison Commission which it replaced.

Relationships and Impressions

I observed and came to share the relationship of cautious mutual respect between administrators and former prison governors, carefully nurtured by

---

1. Lord Windlesham, *Responses to Crime*, Vol 2, *Penal Policy in the Making*, Oxford: Clarendon Press, 1993, page 79.

the Chairman, Arthur Peterson, and my senior administrative colleagues Martin Russell and Norman Storr. Among former prison governors I had particular regard for Duncan Fairn, the Chief Director, and for Hugh Kenyon and Bob Taylor, the Directors of Prison and Borstal Administration respectively. Governors were often under severe pressure (quite a large prison might have only two or three members of the governor grades), and overcrowding was already a problem in local prisons. It was threatening to become a problem in borstals, but the special character of the borstal regime (as it was seen) had to be protected and two new establishments—Everthorpe in East Yorkshire and Stoke Heath in Shropshire—were changed from their intended use as men's training prisons and opened as borstals. I was later to have a particular responsibility for the borstal system—see *Chapter 3*.

It was however a period of confidence and innovation—the establishment of the psychiatric prison at Grendon,[2] and developments in prison regimes such as open prisons, the pre-release employment scheme, pre-release hostels, a special programme in H and K wings at HM Prison Wandsworth, and exciting possibilities at new prisons such as Blundeston—one of the first to be built since the nineteenth century. Psychologists had recently been introduced both to provide psychological services in establishments and especially for the assessment of borstal trainees but also, as Arthur Peterson saw it, to strengthen the professionalism and perhaps the intellectual capacity of the service as a whole. Corporal punishment was still available to visiting committees and boards of visitors[3] as a punishment for serious offences against prison discipline, but it was rarely ordered and never confirmed and

---

2. Grendon was opened in 1962 as an experimental psychiatric prison to provide treatment for prisoners with antisocial personality disorders, under the direction of a medical superintendent. It was later brought more into line with other prisons, with a prison service governor and for a time called a 'psychiatrically supported prison'. It continues to operate a unique therapeutic regime. See for example Elaine Genders and Elaine Player *Grendon: A Study of a Therapeutic Prison*, Oxford University Press 1995.

3. Visiting committees and boards of visitors were independent bodies appointed to supervise the state of prison premises, the administration of prisons and the treatment of prisoners, and at that time to conduct adjudications on offences against prison discipline by prisoners. Visiting committees consisted of and were appointed by local magistrates and served at local prisons which received prisoners from court; boards of visitors were appointed by the Secretary of State and served at all other prison service establishments. Visiting committees were abolished and replaced by boards of visitors in 1967; boards of visitors have now been renamed independent monitoring boards. See *Chapter 3*

it was abolished soon afterwards. 'Restricted diet' (bread and water) was still regularly awarded for quite minor offences.

With Hugh Kenyon I visited a number of prisons, including Leeds, which was at that time the busiest and most over-crowded of the local prisons; Ashwell, a new and pioneering open prison; and Blundeston where I met the men in the special wing for prisoners serving sentences of preventive detention — an indeterminate sentence for offenders with substantial previous records. I was shocked by the length, and cruelty, of the sentences they were serving for quite trivial offences and the injustice which the indeterminate sentence involved. Few new such sentences were being imposed by that time and most of the men I met had been sentenced many years before.

I spent six weeks at Durham Prison as secretary of an inquiry by the visiting committee into a series of allegations of brutality by prison officers and neglect by prison doctors made by a former prisoner. Officers at the prison thought it outrageous that such allegations should be allowed at all, and still more that they should be taken seriously, but there was an uncomfortable feeling at headquarters that there might be something in them. In the event, and to everyone's relief, the inquiry was able honestly to dismiss most of the allegations as trivial or unfounded. In the process I learned a great deal about prison life and prison staff, and gained considerable respect for many prison officers as individuals although the Prison Officers' Association could be assertive and sometimes obstructive, at both national and local levels and especially in later years. See *Chapter 4.*

Prison and Borstal After-Care

My own responsibilities included prison and borstal after-care, prison statistics, the preparation of the Annual Report and enquiries from the press. It fell to me to prepare for prison and borstal welfare and after-care to become a formal responsibility of the Probation Service. The need for more systematic and effective arrangements to prepare prisoners for release and to provide help afterwards had been recognised for some time. The Maxwell report in 1953[4] had brought the problem to notice and had led to the appointment of welfare officers in prisons, but the arrangements were still fragmented

4. *Report of the Committee on Discharged Prisoners' Aid Societies* (the Maxwell report), Cmd 8879, London: HMSO, 1953.

among a range of voluntary organizations with different constitutions and capacities. The great majority of prisoners had to rely on voluntary after-care, provided by a number of local voluntary discharged prisoners' aid societies, who also employed welfare officers in prisons. The Royal London Discharged Prisoners' Aid Society was the largest and most effective; others were of variable quality. 'Voluntary' meant not only that the prisoners could choose whether or not to accept help, but also that the society could choose whether or not to provide it.

Compulsory after-care, with supervision and enforcement of conditions, applied principally to young offenders sentenced to borstal training (see *Chapter 3*), and to adults sentenced to life imprisonment or the special sentences of preventive detention and corrective training. It was the responsibility of the Central After-Care Association (CACA), technically a voluntary organisation but closely linked with the Prison Commission and then the Prison Department. The CACA was organized in three divisions — borstal, men's and women's. The largest and best organized was the borstal division with its origin in the Borstal Association, formed in 1904[5]. Frank Foster was its long-serving, forthright and demanding director. The direct supervision of offenders after release was sometimes provided by the association's own staff, but usually by probation officers acting as its agents. I became its secretary.

The Probation and After-Care Service

A report from the Advisory Council on the Treatment of Offenders[6] had recommended that a specialist section should be formed within the Prison Service, with responsibility for all prison welfare and preparations for release,

5. The Association's papers, now in the National Archives, show that in the period before the First World War known re-offending seems to have been about 25 per cent, but records will have been less reliable and the old borstal population was hardly comparable with young offenders released from prison today. About 25 per cent had gone to sea as merchant seamen (there was a system for them to sign on at Cardiff docks) or had emigrated to the colonies, and a similar proportion were in touch and reported to be doing well. There was no information about the remainder. The files contain personal letters from Edwardian grandees offering positions on their estates or enclosing donations, including one from Herbert Asquith (Prime Minister 1908–1916). See Executive Committee of the Borstal Association: meetings 1-30, 1904–1910 and 31-47, 1910–1918. National Archives, HO 247/97 and 247 /98. Letters to Sir Evelyn Ruggles-Brise, 1897–1935, National Archives HO 247/103.
6. Advisory Council on the Treatment of Offenders (ACTO) *The Organisation of After- Care, Report*, London: HMSO, 1963.

and that the supervision of offenders after release or on probation, should in future be undertaken entirely by the probation service which would be renamed the Probation and After-Care Service. It was decided, probably rightly, that prison welfare officers employed on that basis would be too professionally isolated to be effective and both functions became the responsibility of the Probation and After-Care Service. Local aid societies were disbanded, the Royal London being transformed into the National Association for the Care and Resettlement of Offenders (usually abbreviated to NACRO and later rebranded as Nacro, the crime reduction charity). Probation officers were now, for the first time, to be employed in prisons, although not yet in borstals where preparations for release were still seen as a responsibility of housemasters (as they were called).

There were profound consequences for both the prison and the probation services. For some years afterwards, prison officers felt resentful that what many of them had seen as their most rewarding work had been taken from them, and the change began the process of distancing prison officers from prisoners which gathered momentum with the increased emphasis on security following George Blake's escape from Wormwood Scrubs and the Mountbatten report in 1966 — see *Chapter 3*. For the Probation Service it created tensions between those who valued work in prisons and those who despised it, and was the start of a long and often painful process of adjustment and reform which continued for many years[7]. It had until then been largely a court-based service, dealing mainly with children and young people, and not been much concerned with adult offenders or rates of reoffending, but its workload was growing and the Morison Committee had just (in 1962) made a series of recommendations about recruitment, training and inspection[8].

Over the next few years the service became responsible not only for prison aftercare but also for parole supervision and community service. The work became more demanding and more complex, and much more exposed to scrutiny and criticism. The new service needed and was developing a more outward-looking culture, without the antipathy to prisons and imprisonment

7. See Rob Mawby and Anne Worrall 'They were very threatening about do-gooding bastards: Probation's changing relationships with the police and prison services in England and Wales'. *European Journal of Probation, Vol 3*, No3, 2011, pp 78-94.

8. Home Office *Report of the Departmental Committee on the Probation Service* (The Morison Report), Cmnd 1650, London: HMSO: 1963.

that many probation officers had felt before, and more effective systems of management—issues which the service and the Home Office still had to face when I took responsibility for probation 20 years later—see *Chapter 7*.

After-Care and Rehabilitation

Financial help for prisoners on release had previously been mostly a matter for the local voluntary discharged prisoners' aid society. It was often a charitable and discretionary gift of about half a crown (now about £5), accompanied by a homily on gratitude and the need to stay out of trouble in future. After protracted negotiations with the National Assistance Board and the Treasury, we introduced a standard discharge grant of £1 to which all prisoners were entitled. It is now £46, about the same value as it was then, but the transitional problems of financial support and access to benefits for people leaving prison, especially if they are homeless, seem to be as difficult now as they were in 1964.

The increasing interest in prisoner's welfare and after-care reflected a growing, if usually unspoken, recognition of the damage that a prison sentence can do both to the prisoner and to his or her family. Voluntary organisations were being set up to provide services such as accommodation for prisoners after release: examples included New Bridge, Norman Houses, St Vincent de Paul, the Blackfriars Settlement and the Stonham Housing Association. Lord Longford and Lord Stonham were among the politicians who gave their support. Parliamentary debates were mostly about how more could be done to help offenders and improve prison conditions[9]. Compassion for those in difficulty extended beyond prisoners and prisoners: a colleague at the National Assistance Board told me at the time that it was considered more important to ensure that claimants received the full amounts to which they were entitled than to detect and punish fraud.

The attention given to prison after-care might seem comparable with the Coalition government's commitment to rehabilitation and a 'rehabilitation revolution', but there are two differences. One is that support for after-care

---

9.   Two examples among many others are the debates in the House of Lords on 21 April 1958 (Official Report vol 208 cc 912-989), and 1 April 1963 (vol 248 cc 373-438). Henry Brooke as Home Secretary was keen to announce the introduction of the prisoners' discharge grant before the 1964 election because he thought it would help the Conservative Party's chances of re-election.

was founded on a belief that most prisoners had some capacity for good and needed help to achieve it: if prisoners and their families could be helped towards better and more law-abiding lives, that needed no further justification. In contrast, the 'rehabilitation revolution' seems to start from the assumption that prisoners are 'bad people' and its purpose is not to benefit prisoners as people but to protect the public from them. The other is that the 'rehabilitation revolution' seems to be inseparably connected with a commercial model and 'payment by results', with no visible philanthropic element.

I was pleased to feel part of what seemed at that time to be a progressive movement. I had not then seen the darker side of imprisonment which Terence and Pauline Morris exposed in their sociological study of Pentonville at about the same time,[10] but I remember the concern and disbelief which their report caused among my senior colleagues and I saw its impact on the sometimes wishful thinking that was prevalent at the time. Its influence on the Prison Service continued for many years — see Alison Liebling's appreciation of the Study and Terence Morris's own recollections published in the *Prison Service Journal*.[11] I am sorry that I did not until many years later become more familiar with the work on deviance and social control by scholars such as Jock Young and Stan Cohen who were then becoming established at the London School of Economics.

The prison population during that period was about 28,000.

Four Jobs In Four Years 1966-1970

I then spent shorter but memorable periods dismantling most of the arrangements for civil defence (they would no longer have been effective against the type of nuclear attack which by then seemed to be a possibility); and working with Lord Shackleton, the leader of the House of Lords, and with Michael Wheeler-Booth[12] on the Wilson government's attempt to reform the House of Lords in 1967-1968[13].

---

10. Terence and Pauline Morris *Pentonville: A Sociological Study of an English Prison*, London: Routledge, 1963.
11. Alison Liebling 'Pentonville Revisited: An Essay in Honour of the Morrises' Sociological Study of an English Prison, 1958-1963' and Terence Morris 'A Lifetime with Pentonville', both in the *Prison Service Journal*, September 2013, No 209, pages 29-35 and 36-42.
12. A House of Lords Clerk, later Clerk of the Parliaments.
13. For a recent study, see Chris Ballinger *The House of Lords 1911-2011: A Century of Non-Reform*. Oxford, Hart, 2012.

There followed a period in the Northern Ireland Division (as it then was) and in Northern Ireland itself at the time when troops were first deployed on the streets of Belfast and Londonderry in August 1968. I soon came to realise the extent to which Westminster governments had ignored Northern Ireland over the previous 45 years, and had seen the situation entirely through the eyes of the protestant, Unionist government. The reasons were clear enough — the Conservative Party was closely identified with the Ulster Unionist Party and the Labour Party had no presence or organization in the province, so that the catholic population had no effective representation either in Northern Ireland or at Westminster. Few people at Westminster or in Whitehall had any clear understanding of Northern Ireland's history, social situation or the extent of the oppression that was then taking place.[14] In the Home Office, Northern Ireland was the responsibility of a principal (grade 7) who also covered the Channel Islands and the Isle of Man, and whose main task had been to secure favourable treatment for Northern Ireland in matters of United Kingdom agricultural and industrial policy. It was emphatically not to ask awkward questions about the policies (still less the legitimacy) of the Northern Ireland government.

Part of my job, apart from responding to what were then fast-moving events, was to produce regular commentaries on the situation, known as 'Home Office Northern Ireland Information Papers', and more generally to try to create a better understanding of the sensibilities of the two communities and of what was happening and what was at stake. I relied in the first place on a Quaker study[15] which seemed to be the only independent source of information that was available at that time. I accompanied James Callaghan, the Home Secretary, at his meeting with Harold Wilson when the decision was first taken to send in the troops, and on the way back we wondered whether they would stay for a few months or for as long as four or five years. I also spent some weeks in Northern Ireland as political adviser to the General Officer Commanding, Lt General Freeland, visiting troubled areas such as the Falls Road in Belfast and the Bogside in Londonderry and

---

14. Ministers visiting from Northern Ireland were astonished that someone with a Catholic name — Patricia Murphy — could be allowed to work in the Home Secretary's private office.

15. Denis Barritt and Arthur Booth, *Orange and Green: A Quaker Study of Community Relations in Northern Ireland,* prepared for the Northern Friends Peace Board of the Religious Society of Friends (Quakers), 1969.

making contact with sections of the community such as the trades unions[16] whose voice was not often heard.

In October 1968 I was appointed as James Callaghan's private secretary. I admired him for his work in Northern Ireland, and it was a tragedy that his reforms of policing, housing and employment could not take effect in time to forestall the violence which followed. I also admired him for his part in bringing about the final abolition of capital punishment for murder, although most of the heavy lifting had been done by others beforehand. I was for a time in two minds about his decision to ask the MCC to call off the South African cricket tour. Callaghan's instinct was that the tour ought to be cancelled, but he was influenced by the argument that politics and sport should be kept separate and he justified his decision not as a protest against apartheid but on grounds of the threat to public order and the ability of the police to control the demonstrations that were expected. It was the right decision but its justification made the government look weak and may have contributed to the Labour Party's defeat in the 1970 election. What I did find hard to accept was what I thought to be his inhuman treatment of refugees from East Africa and his attempts to drive them away when they tried to gain admission to this country. It was the period when he was preoccupied with his differences with the Prime Minister Harold Wilson over Barbara Castle's white paper *In Place of Strife* on the future of the trades unions and industrial relations. He was suspicious and secretive, and I found it very difficult to communicate with him.

A Period of Liberal Reform?

The 1960s were a period of liberal reform — the Race Relations Acts of 1965 and 1968; the Sexual Offences Act 1967; the Children and Young Persons Act 1969, with its emphasis on the interests of the child; the Divorce Reform Act 1969; the suspension and then abolition of capital punishment for murder; the establishment of the Law Commission and the Parliamentary Commissioner for Administration (the Ombudsman); and the admittedly unsuccessful attempt to reform the House of Lords. The reforms marked a change in the character of British society which is still continuing today.

---

16. Trades unions were organized on an all-Ireland basis and were one of the few institutions which were not established on a sectarian basis.

They were associated especially with the personalities of Roy Jenkins as Home Secretary and Lord Gardiner as Lord Chancellor. Most of them were unusual at the time in being promoted through Private Members' Bills rather than the government's own legislation. It is hard to say how far they affected the character of the Home Office itself, but—perhaps more slowly than we should have done—we became more aware of, and more sensitive towards, issues of equality in respect of race, gender and religion; and we realised more clearly that race relations involved more than controlling immigration, as had sometimes been supposed.

The 1960s were also a time of increasing restrictions on immigration, especially from the Commonwealth; racial tensions; public disorder, often arising from demonstrations against the war in Vietnam and culminating in the disturbance in Grosvenor Square in 1968; and corruption in the Metropolitan Police and Sir Robert Mark's action to correct it. The government and the prison and probation services began to lose confidence in the optimistic vision set out in *Penal Practice in a Changing Society* and in the effectiveness of prisons and probation in preventing and reducing crime. In 1962 the government set up a Royal Commission on the Penal System, and abolished the Advisory Council on the Treatment of Offenders (ACTO) at the same time. In the event, the Royal Commission failed to make progress and was eventually abandoned. There have been various accounts and different views of the reasons, but they included disagreement among its members, and the fact that the Labour government which came into office in 1964 had its own ideas and did not want to wait for the commission's report.[17] The Prison Service was humiliated by the escape of George Blake from Wormwood Scrubs Prison in 1964 and convulsed by the Mountbatten inquiry which followed.[18]

There was also a loss of confidence in the Civil Service and especially in and among what was then called the 'First Division' or the 'Administrative Class'. It was reflected in the report of the Fulton Commission[19] and the

---

17.   One account is in Leon Radzinowicz's *Adventures in Criminology*, London: Routledge 1999, pages 333-352.

18.   Home Office *Report of the Inquiry into Prison Escapes and Security* (The Mountbatten Report), Cmnd 3175, London: HMSO, 1966.

19.   Lord Fulton *The Civil Service: Report of the Committee* (the Fulton Report), London: HMSO, 1968.

commission's criticism of its lack of scientific and economic training. It could be connected with C P Snow's influential criticism of what he saw as the damaging effect of the 'Two Cultures',[20] one based on the arts or humanities and the other on science, and the lack of scientific knowledge among the country's supposed intellectual elite. Many of us thought the criticism unfair, but it was impossible to say so in public without appearing complacent and self-satisfied.[21] The argument ebbed and flowed, and later took a new direction with the Conservative government's Financial Management Initiative and its emphasis on economy, efficiency and effectiveness and on quantified and measurable results — see *Chapter 5* onwards. The tension continues today in the relationship between justice and humanity on the one hand and performance and delivery on the other, but it is rarely discussed.

As the Conservative government took office in 1970, I sensed that the political and social environment would be more troubled and more demanding in the 1970s than it had been when I joined the Home Office ten years before, and so it proved to be

---

20. C P Snow, *The Two Cultures*, Cambridge University Press, 1959.
21. I was interested, and pleased, to see the recent revival of F. R. Leavis's criticism of that thesis — F R Leavis *The Two Cultures? The significance of C. P. Snow*, with an Introduction by *Stephan Collini*, Cambridge University Press, 2013.

CHAPTER 3

Borstals, Detention Centres and Women's Prisons

Following the change of government in 1970, I returned to the Prison Department as head of the division (P4) which was concerned with young offenders, women and girls and prisoners on remand. The division also had responsibility for the appointment and functions of members of boards of visitors (now independent monitoring boards (IMBs)), including their then role in adjudications for offences against prison discipline.

What Had to be Done

The Prison Service was still recovering from the escape of George Blake from Wormwood Scrubs Prison and was concentrating on implementing the Mountbatten report. In adult men's prisons security was necessarily all-important and treatment and training, or rehabilitation, were secondary. The prison population had grown rapidly during the 1960s, and prisons were now acutely overcrowded. A system of 'tactical management' had been introduced to spread the pressure more evenly across the system, mainly by regular and often extremely disruptive 'overcrowding drafts' to transfer prisoners from more crowded to less crowded prisons. Other parts of the prison system, such as establishments for young offenders received less attention. Apart from the rebuilding of Holloway Prison—see below—the idealistic hopes of the early-1960s had given way to grim realism.

The Prison Service was also coming under what many of its members felt to be subversive criticism from an unaccustomed direction—from prisoners' representatives and prisoners themselves. The Union for the Preservation of the Rights of Prisoners (PROP) demanded recognition as the equivalent of a prisoners' trade union, and Radical Alternatives to Prison (RAP) called for the abolition of imprisonment altogether. They had a point of view to which I thought the Prison Department should listen and if possible respond, but even in those days, when hostility to any talk of prisoners' rights was not as emotional as it later became,[1] it would have been hard politically to be seen to be making 'concessions'. The service generally was still defensive in its response to any criticism, but some of us began to make contact with the interest groups which were then being formed, and to have constructive discussions with them. The Advisory Council on the Penal System had been appointed to replace the Advisory Council on the Treatment of Offenders but with wider terms of reference, and it was now carrying out a review of the sentencing and custodial arrangements for young offenders.

My division's main tasks were to modernise the custodial system for young offenders, keeping in touch with the Advisory Council's review; to rebuild Holloway prison; and to improve the conditions for unconvicted prisoners and if possible reduce their number. Others were to overhaul the arrangements for boards of visitors and clarify their role, and improve the conduct of prison adjudications.

None of those was a political priority for ministers, and the senior officials who formed the Prisons Board were still preoccupied with giving effect to the Mountbatten report on prison security and the issues associated with high security men's prisons. The result was that my colleagues and I had considerable freedom of manoeuvre, and were for the most part left to get on with whatever we wanted to do. We wrote reports for an elaborate, Treasury-led, programme known as 'Policy Analysis and Review', but we had little or no reaction to them from the Prisons Board, still less from ministers. I had an excellent relationship with Terry Weiler, my immediate boss, but I cannot remember meeting a minister at any time during that period, or the chairman of the Prisons Board (at first William Pile, later Robert Cox) on more than one or two occasions. Published accounts of what we did can be found in the contributions I wrote for the Prison Department's annual reports. I began a practice of setting ourselves some targets (mostly dates by which things had to be done) which were then unusual in the Prison Service or the Home Office.

Borstals and Young Offenders

Borstal institutions and the sentence of borstal training had been formally established by the Prevention of Crime Act 1907, for young offenders aged

---

1.   For example over the right to vote in elections.

15-21 (for a time 15-23) for whom the courts thought there was some prospect of reform.[2] The sentence at that time was one of two years with a minimum of six months in custody and the remainder under supervision, the date of release being decided, effectively, by the borstal staff. They were modelled on the English public school system, with houses, house masters and matrons, and staff wore plain clothes. During the 1930s the prison commissioner Sir Alexander Paterson had developed a vision of borstal training which had inspired a previous generation of governors and housemasters (as assistant governors were called), and for many years they had been considered a great success, due partly to their selective intake. There was such confidence in the system that it had become the principal custodial sentence for young offenders and since the Criminal Justice Act 1967 the only medium-term sentence that was available for them.

My first contact with the borstal system had been as a student in Oxford in 1954. The eccentric but deeply committed governor of Huntercombe Borstal, Sir Almeric Rich, Bart., used to arrange for some of the trainees to catch the bus into Oxford on Saturday afternoons where they were met and entertained by members of the university society Crime a Challenge. Sadly, the society was disbanded when Oxford Prison was closed (to become a luxury hotel) and as students' interests changed and the academic pressures upon them became more intense. I do not know how far this old-fashioned and elitist practice was of any benefit to either trainees or students, but the trainees enjoyed what was usually a visit to the cinema and a meal in an inexpensive restaurant, and students were helped to realise that offenders are human beings like anyone else.

The service had built up an elaborate process of classification and allocation to specialised institutions based on a psychological assessment of the individual's personality-type. Research by Hermann Mannheim and Leslie Wilkins, and later by Roger Hood[3] and then by Vernon Holloway, had shown that an offender's subsequent progress could be more or less accurately predicted by

---

2.   If the court was 'satisfied having regard to his character and previous conduct, and to the circumstances of the offence, that it is expedient for his reformation and the prevention of crime that he should undergo a period of training in a borstal institution'.

3.   Hermann Mannheim and Leslie Wilkins 'Prediction methods in relation to Borstal training', *Studies in the Causes of Delinquency and the Treatment of Offenders,* London: HMSO, 1955; Roger Hood, *Borstal Reassessed,* London, Heinemann, 1965.

reference to his history and background at the time of sentence, regardless
of the type of institution or regime to which they might subsequently be
allocated. It had become clear that the allocation process was wasteful and
no longer served any useful purpose[4].

Detention centres had originally been introduced under the Criminal
Justice Act 1948 as a 'short, sharp shock' to replace corporal punishment. There was at first a strong emphasis on the punitive aspects of the
regime—drill, inspections, strict discipline—which appealed to the courts
and to most politicians at the time. That emphasis was found to encourage
a culture of bullying and brutality and by the early 1960s the service had
developed a more positive training regime resembling that in borstals, but
by then detention centres no longer had a sufficient identity of their own
to justify a separate type of institution or a separate sentence. The separate
sentences of detention in a detention centre, borstal training and imprisonment no longer made sense, either to the courts or to the Prison Service,
although the Conservative Party remained attached to detention centres
until the mid-1980s.

Pressures and Criticisms

Like prisons, borstals and detention centres were under severe pressure of
numbers. In borstals the situation was managed by holding trainees for
long periods at the allocation centres at Manchester and Wormwood Scrubs
Prisons until vacancies became available in 'training' borstals themselves.
For detention centres, courts were asked to enquire whether a vacancy was
available before making a detention centre order and to consider another
sentence if not. Both situations were deeply unsatisfactory.

Most of those concerned with the system, including judges and magistrates, had come to agree that the fixed but indeterminate borstal sentence
had become a source of serious injustice. It allowed no room for flexibility
for the courts to recognise different degrees of culpability and the arrangements for assessing progress and dates of release could be manipulated by
borstal staff. Neither the sentence nor the regime was suited to the social
circumstances of the 1960s and 1970s or to the more street-wise and criminally sophisticated young people who were receiving borstal sentences at that

---

4.   There were separate arrangements for the much smaller number of young women.

time. Trainees still mostly conformed to the regime, but they did not often appreciate or benefit from the experience as their predecessors might have done (or were claimed to have done). Some governors complained nostalgically about the decline in the quality of the trainees they were receiving, but many governors and most assistant governors realised that the time had come for a change both in the assumptions that were made and in the practices that were followed.

Modernisation and Normalisation

We tried in various ways to make the experience of borstal less artificial and more relevant to the trainees' ordinary lives, and to emphasise doing things 'with' rather than 'to' or 'for' them. They were to be treated with dignity and respect as people, with lives and responsibilities of their own, and not stereotyped as offenders or trainees. We simplified the arrangements for allocation to the different institutions and eliminated the delays which the process had involved. We tried various innovations to connect borstal institutions more closely with their surrounding communities and with the communities from which their trainees were drawn.

One example was a hostel in Ipswich at which trainees from Hollesley Bay Borstal could spend part of their sentences and work for local employers. I would have liked more to be established, but they were difficult and expensive to staff and manage, and also doubts about their legal status, and they eventually fell victim to restrictions on staff overtime.

Another project was the two 'neighbourhood' borstals at Hindley in Greater Manchester and Hewell Grange in the West Midlands whose trainees were allocated there because they lived in the surrounding area and not as previously because they fitted a certain type of personality. Drawing on the experience of Andrew Rutherford's workshops at Everthorpe Borstal, special arrangements were made with the probation and other local services to keep trainees in touch with their families and to introduce to or re-connect them with the opportunities for work, education and health care which could be made available to them after release. A unique feature was the formation of joint teams of probation officers and prison officers who stayed together and worked with the trainees inside the institution and then in the community when they were under supervision after release. The Probation Services involved were particularly enthusiastic but the scheme was later abandoned because it could not be reconciled with the demands of the tactical management of the prison population and the need to fill places wherever they could be found.

An interesting test was whether trainees should be allowed to grow their hair long, as was the fashion for young men at that time, or whether they should be required and if necessary forced to have it cut short as part of their punishment. My colleagues and I preferred the former, subject to the requirements of health and safety, as part of the 'normalisation' of borstal training and a mark of respect for the person's identity and choice, and incidentally because cutting a person's hair forcibly would probably constitute an assault. Some staff found that difficult to accept, regarding long hair as a challenge to their authority. We did not want to provoke a confrontation which might have excited the *Daily Mail*, and good sense eventually prevailed, although not until one trainee had spent most of his sentence in the borstal hospital where officers would not be offended by his appearance. It was not a matter on which we thought we needed to trouble ministers.

The Wider Context

We worked closely with the Advisory Council on the Penal System in its review of the custodial and non-custodial arrangements for young offenders. The interaction between the council's deliberations and the developments which were taking place on the ground seemed especially productive at the time, although critics such as Mick Ryan[5] might say that the relationship was too cosy, elitist and exclusive. The council shared our scepticism about the value of specialised institutions catering for different levels of intelligence and types of personality, and thought it more important that trainees should so far as possible stay within easy reach of their home areas, both to keep in touch with their families and to prepare for their lives after release. Their eventual report,[6] with its recommendations for a single sentence and for establishments to be organized so that a full range of facilities could so far as possible be provided on a single site serving its local area, was very much

5.   Mick Ryan *Penal Policy and Political Culture in England and Wales,* Sherfield-on-Loddon: Waterside Press, 2003.

6.   Advisory Council on the Penal System, *Young Adult Offenders,* London: HMSO, 1974.

as I expected and hoped but its implementation proved to be a long drawn out business. There were increasing pressures of overcrowding on the prison system as a whole; the prison building programme was abandoned because of the country's financial difficulties; and the Probation Service was preoccupied with the introduction of community service following the council's earlier report, inspired by Barbara Wootton, on Non-Custodial and Semi-Custodial Penalties,[7] and at the same time with other initiatives such as the introduction of day training centres, intensive supervision schemes and an expansion of hostels. It was an exciting time for the Probation Service, and understandable that arrangements for young offenders serving custodial sentences should not be its first priority.[8] The sentencing structure for young offenders was eventually reformed by the Criminal Justice Acts of 1982 and 1988, but a more local organization of establishments is an aspiration which has always been out of reach. Attempts to enable prisoners, of all kinds, to serve their sentences in prisons nearer to their home areas were reinforced by the Woolf report in 1991 and have continued since then, but they were and still are frustrated by financial pressures and operational constraints.

Colleagues elsewhere in the Prison Department felt strongly that the professional identity and skills of prison staff lay in the management of secure institutions and in keeping them safe and secure, and that involvement with communities was at best an indulgence which the service could not afford and at worst a dangerous distraction. There was also a sense that young offender institutions, and especially borstals, enjoyed an unfairly privileged position in the prison system as a whole. The progress we made was always precarious, and the balance was later changed to the point where young adults became arguably the most neglected section of the prison population.

During that period, Dr Alec Dickson, the founder and director of Community Service Volunteers, and Elisabeth Hoodless came to see me with a proposal that in order to relieve the pressure CSV should itself provide and run a borstal institution. They said it would be a simple operation, they would be able to set it up very quickly, and CSV were already providing

---

7. Advisory Council on the Penal System, *Non-Custodial and Semi-Custodial Penalties*, London: HMSO, 1970.

8. For an insightful personal account of the introduction and early development of community service in England and Wales, see John Harding 'Forty Years On: A celebration of community service by offenders', *Probation Journal*, 60(3) 325-331, 2013.

places on their programmes for borstal trainees who were approaching the time for their release. I liked the idea of the kind of institution that CSV would provide and I was not at that time troubled by 'outsourcing' (as it would now be called) as a matter of principle. But it would be a major new venture, needing not only the approval of my senior colleagues and ministers but also legislation and legislative vehicles did not pass by as regularly as they did in later years. I was sorry that I had to give Alec Dickson a discouraging answer, with which he was clearly disappointed. It was an idea 30 years ahead of its time.

Women and Girls

We tried to apply similar principles to women and girls. It was generally easier to do so — women were, for example, already allowed to wear their own clothes, although with some differences of view about what kinds of clothes (for example trousers) were or were not acceptable, with different practices at different prisons. A difficult issue, not spoken of more than we could help, was whether lesbian relationships could be acknowledged and tolerated as they were at Holloway, or rigorously suppressed as they were at Styal. In the circumstances of the time it seemed better not to press the issue to a confrontation, to deal sensitively with particular cases as they arose, and to allow good sense, humanity and changing public opinion to prevail, as they eventually did.

A difficult issue arose over prisoners who insisted on using the Welsh language, especially those charged with disorder at Welsh nationalist demonstrations. Prison officers could not bear the loss of control they thought they suffered when they could not read letters or understand conversations. There was not a problem for men at Cardiff or Swansea where there were Welsh-speaking officers and a more relaxed attitude towards the Welsh language generally, but women had to go to Pucklechurch in England where officers saw the use of Welsh not as the exercise of a legitimate right but as a challenge to their authority. Various devices were used to prevent a confrontation, and again good sense eventually prevailed.

Myra Hindley was at Holloway Prison for much of that time. Her treatment presented a special problem for staff, not only because of what she had done[9] but also because she was a devious and manipulative woman. Her life could always be in danger from other prisoners, and the press would inevitably exploit any story that could be told about her. Lord Longford took a close interest in Hindley and believed she had become a reformed woman who might in time be released; that was thought be impossible, for her own safety if for no other reason, but his concern for her, even if some people thought it naïve, was treated with respect. It was sad that Dorothy Wing's compassionate but ill-judged decision to take her for a walk on Hampstead Heath ended the career of a dedicated and humane governor.

The women's service was still separate from the rest of the Prison Service at that time, with exclusively male staff in men's prisons and young establishments for young offenders[10] and exclusively female staff in those for women. The process of integration began nervously and tentatively with the posting of two male officers from Pentonville to Holloway. They were confined to security duties at the gate, they were not allowed to enter the women's accommodation, and the arrangement only lasted a short time. A more serious step forward was the posting of women assistant governors to two men's borstals, and a process of more general integration grew from that.

Rebuilding Holloway Prison

The decision to rebuild Holloway had been taken some time before I returned to the Prison Department. Joanna Kelley, the women's director and a former governor of Holloway, and William Pile as chairman of the Prisons Board, had persuaded the board and ministers that they should give effect to her idealistic vision of Holloway as a secure hospital, while remaining the system's largest and principal women's establishment. The prison was to be rebuilt on its existing site and it was to stay in full operation, although with reduced numbers, while rebuilding took place. The design and building work were not to be undertaken by the Directorate of Works, who normally managed prison building projects and had the relevant experience, but the directorate disapproved of the whole idea and the work was contracted-out to private

9.   With Ian Brady she had murdered several children and buried their bodies on Saddleworth Moor. An account of Hindley's walk on Hampstead Heath appears in Joanna Kozubska *Cries for Help: Women's Imprisonment in the 1970s, Myra Hindley and Her Contemporaries* (2014), Sherfield-on-Loddon: Waterside Press.

10. Apart from the 'matrons' who were employed in borstals.

architects chosen for their expertise in designing hospitals and to private firms of quantity surveyors and other specialists. A small and inexperienced team had been assembled in P4 Division to prepare the design brief and manage the project within the department. I was told firmly that we must at all costs retain our credibility with the Treasury, and must therefore keep rigidly to the cost limits that had been agreed with them. It all felt very precarious, but it was what had been decided and the vision was one which I thought I could share. I described the scheme's vision and its intentions in paper for the *Howard Journal*[11] in which I wrote

> The central features of the new establishment will be its medical, surgical and psychiatric facilities and its community life. This concept reflects the growing recognition that .most women and girls in custody need some form of medical, psychiatric or remedial treatment and some form of training to help them live in a community. Most of them are inadequate in one way or another, and many of them are highly disturbed. On the other hand, there are few who could be described as professional or hardened criminals and very few need a high degree of security. There may be waves of hysteria or demonstrations of aggression — towards themselves, towards property, or towards each other or the staff — but few women have the resources or the wish to organise a major disturbance or a serious attempt to escape. Those who are violent in prison are not usually violent outside and their violence is commonly an outburst which reflects an inability to express themselves in other ways...

> There will throughout be an attempt to develop her resources in a way which seems likely to help her in the future — by improving her ability to communicate, by giving her practical skills which might help her to earn her living, by encouraging spare-time interests which will keep her occupied during her leisure time, and by letting her know where in the community she can look for help if she needs it...

> The new establishment is being designed not only for the inmates but also for the staff. Both will be members of its community and the staff will generally be members for a good deal longer than the inmates. One objective already

---

11. 'The Redevelopment of Holloway Prison', *Howard Journal of Penology and Crime Prevention*, XIII/2, 122-132, 1971.

mentioned is to encourage all members of the staff to work as a single therapeutic team. Another is to improve their working and living environment so that their relationships with inmates can be more relaxed and so that they can have greater self-confidence and self-respect both in the establishment and outside it ... The new quarters have been designed to be part of the surrounding district and not merely an addition to the main establishment. Life for the staff should be as natural as is possible within an institutional setting, both for their own sake and for the sake of the inmates, and partly for this reason it is hoped to include a larger proportion of male officers ...

The design [of the prison] will seek to give an impression of normality and to remove the impressions of mystery and terror which have been associated with so many prisons in the past.

In the event the vision proved unrealistic. The 'medical model' of penal treatment on which it was based soon became discredited; the assumptions about the future size and nature of the women's prison population proved to be mistaken (an estimate at the time was that it would fall to about 800 and remain at that level—it is now over 4,000); the support which the staff seemed to show during what was thought to be a careful and inclusive process of consultation was not sustained when staff had moved on and the disruption of rebuilding began to take effect. In order to keep within the cost limits I agreed that the corridors should be narrowed and the ceilings lowered, a mistake from which staff and prisoners have suffered ever since. I eventually had to ask that the Directorate of Works, with its much greater resources and professional skills, should after all take over the management of the building work, but other problems remained—the weakness of the original concept, the disruption of trying to rebuild the prison while keeping it in full operation, the unexpected rise in the women's population, and the demands for special security for prisoners who were Irish terrorists. The subsequent story has been told by Paul Rock and Elaine Player.[12]

---

12. Paul Rock *Reconstructing a Women's Prison: The Holloway Redevelopment Project, 1968-1988*, Oxford: Oxford University Press, 1996; Elaine Player 'Prisons' policy: the redevelopment of Holloway Prison' in David Downes, Dick Hobbs and Tim Newburn (eds.), *The Eternal Recurrence of Crime and Control*, Oxford University Press, 2010, pages 95-114.

In retrospect I have to accept that the Holloway project was an example of bad decision-making and bad implementation, for example in the use of evidence, the process of consultation, the management capacity to deliver the project and the need for sustained commitment and support from the Prison Department and the Prison Service as whole. Perhaps we were also too ready to look for and listen to only the evidence we wanted to hear. I have many times asked myself whether our vision of the new Holloway was fundamentally flawed and the nature of prisons always makes it impossible to run them in the way we hoped; or whether it was sound but the Prison Service was not yet culturally able to adjust to it and might in time have done so with better preparation and support from management.

Other Initiatives

Two other ventures are worth recalling from that time. One was an attempt to reduce the number of defendants who were sent to prison on remand, partly to relieve overcrowding but also as a matter of natural justice, especially when many of them did not in the event receive prison sentences. We promoted the first bail hostel, initially provided and run by the Salvation Army and the precursor to the much larger, mainstream programme run by the Probation Service. We experimented with 'bail information schemes', which aimed to give prisoners information and help in preparing their applications for bail and which in later years became normal practice; and we tried unsuccessfully to arrange for prison medical reports to be prepared for courts on an 'out-patient' basis to avoid the need for a remand in custody if that was its only purpose.

The other was our work with boards of visitors. Our aim was to make them more independent and more effective, and to bring a greater degree of procedural justice and legitimacy to the administration of prisons. We were especially concerned about the conduct of adjudications for offences against prison discipline, for which we introduced training and guidance and I believe brought about a real improvement. It was not however enough to overcome the more fundamental objections to the disciplinary role of those boards—their lack of independence from the management of the institution, the potential conflict between their different roles, the severity of the punishments they could impose through the loss of remission (equivalent in many cases to the imposition of a substantial new sentence), the lack of legal advice, the absence of a satisfactory means of appeal. After much debate, several legal challenges and an inconclusive formal review, their disciplinary function was eventually abolished following a recommendation in the Woolf report.[13] The issue of legitimacy in prisons and in criminal justice more generally grew in significance in later years and became the subject of important work by scholars including Richard Sparks, Anthony Bottoms, Tom Tyler[14] and others.

It was during that period that I came to see the value of conferences and seminars as opportunities to share experiences and ideas. They were a means of improving communication, making connections, and encouraging lateral thinking. They could make a valuable contribution to the formation of policy at a stage before it became crystallised as specific proposals, and help to generate a sense of shared ownership for proposals when they emerged.

The prison population in 1974 was about 40,000.

---

13. Lord Justice Woolf (1991) *Report of an Inquiry into the Prison Disturbances of April 1990*, Cmnd 1456, London: HMSO, 1991.
14. Richard Sparks, Anthony Bottoms and Will Hay *Prisons and the Problem of Order*, Oxford University Press, 1996; Anthony Bottoms, 'Compliance and community penalties' in Anthony Bottoms, Lorraine Gelsthorpe and Sue Rex (eds.), *Community Penalties: Change and Challenge*, Cullompton: Willan, 2001; Tom Tyler, *Why People Obey the Law: Procedural Justice, Legitimacy and Compliance*, Princeton University Press, 2006.

CHAPTER 4

Prisons in Crisis

Prisons and the May Report

After postings to the Establishments Department (see *Chapter 10*), the Police Department and the Cabinet Office, I returned to the Home Office at the beginning of 1980 where William Whitelaw was now Home Secretary. My immediate task was to obtain decisions on the recommendations of the May Committee's report on the Prison Service,[1] and then to put them into effect. The review had been set up primarily to resolve a complicated dispute over prison officers' pay but it had been extended to cover the Prison Service more generally. My own responsibilities were for those recommendations which related to the structure of the Prison Department and its regional offices and the appointment of an independent chief inspector of prisons. The recommendations on pay were dealt with separately, and their lack of clarity caused the dispute to drag on for another two years.

The questions of structure had two aspects. One was the relationship between headquarters, regional offices and prison establishments, and the other was the relationship between 'policy' and 'operations' in the arrangements for the service's governance. Underlying both was the long-running competition for power between Prison Department headquarters (from which the service often distanced itself, calling it the 'Home Office') and the 'operational' prison staff (governors and prison officers) working in prisons together with the four regional directors.

Regional directors' offices had been progressively enlarged over the previous few yew years, resulting in what the May Committee found to be considerable duplication of effort and the creation of alternative and competing centres of power and influence. Regional directors often operated in idiosyncratic ways, there were inconsistencies between regions, and they had different reputations among their Prison Service colleagues. They had taken

---

1. Home Office *Committee of Inquiry into the United Kingdom Prison Services* (the May Committee), Cmnd 7673, London: HMSO, 1979.

full charge of young offenders' and women's establishments in their regions and the post of women's director had been abolished. The report recommended that regional offices should be reduced in size and in the scope of their responsibilities, but any proposal for a reduction was regarded by many people as an attack on the Prison Service itself. In the event some savings were made, some compromises were accepted and a more or less amicable settlement was reached, but nothing much changed until the structure was radically overhauled and regional directors were replaced by a larger number of area managers in the late-1980s.

Another problem, which the review had not addressed, was the unequal balance between the workloads of the four regional directors and their offices, and the difficulty which that caused both for management and professional leadership. It was most serious in London and the south-east, especially in respect of women's prisons (including Holloway) now that there was no longer a director for women and it remained unresolved for several more years. I would have liked to propose a more radical scheme of regionalisation in which most prisoners apart from those needing the highest security could serve their sentences in their home areas and the regions could develop a stronger sense of identity with the communities they served and some accountability towards them. A development of that kind was however considered impractical, as it always has been, because of the uneven distribution of prison establishments across the country, and because operational pressures, management culture and political indifference have so far made it impossible to translate a vision of that kind into a practical reality.

A different and more subtle question concerned what I saw as the relationship within the Prison Department between policy and operations or, as I preferred to see it, the balance between the interests of the Secretary of State and those of the Prison Service itself. The former were essentially the national interest,[2] taking account of the political realities of the time but going beyond the personal and political interests of ministers themselves. The latter were what later came dismissively to be called 'provider interests', but they included the conditions considered necessary for the orderly functioning of prisons and the wellbeing of prisoners and staff, together with the

---

2.   The definition and interpretation of the 'national interest' as it affects civil servants became the subject of the Armstrong Memorandum: see *Chapter 11*.

changes which staff wished to make and the activities they wished to carry on as matters of their own professional judgement.

Most of the time the two sets of interests coincided; occasionally they did not. The tension between them had been, and was still, managed by the appointment to the Prison Department of administrative or Treasury grade civil servants whose role was to look after the interests of the Secretary of State, to work alongside prison governors and former prison governors who would represent the interests of the service itself and its institutions. Any disagreement or conflict would be resolved at the Prisons Board or by reference to ministers. In practice, we usually worked amicably together as colleagues, respecting each other's experience and point of view and trying to do the best we could in the situation in which we were placed.

That situation had been understood and respected when I was serving in the Prison Department 15 and again ten years before, but it was now becoming blurred. Increasing numbers of governors were now being appointed to headquarters to do jobs which were indistinguishable from those of administrators, and they had a reasonable complaint that no governor had so far been able to reach the position of head of their own service.[3] The Director General, Dennis Trevelyan, had a 'normal' Home Office administrative background, but for ten years since the Mountbatten report the appointment had been made from outside the Home Office altogether, and the person appointed had no previous experience either of prisons or the criminal justice sector.

The solution I recommended was the creation of a post as deputy director general and the service's operational head, to be occupied by Gordon Fowler, its most senior and highly respected former governor, and alongside it but at a lower level a new administrative post of Director of Operational Policy. Both would be members of the Prisons Board and both would report to the Director General. As a gesture, regional directors also became members of the Prisons Board, as well as their line manager the deputy director general, so that people with operational experience would now form a majority. Other 'administrative' directors were John Chilcot and Ken Neale, and Tim Flesher was the Board's secretary. There were no women, but Jenny Hughes was later appointed as a non-executive director from a business background and she became a valued colleague.

---

3. Richard Tilt became the first governor to reach that position when he was appointed in 1995.

I saw the Director of Operational Policy as having responsibility for a number of well-established administrative functions, and as providing the 'outward looking' face of the service with its sights pointing towards ministers, Whitehall and Westminster, and interpreting the wider political and administrative environment to the board and to the service in the field. It was thus the point at which 'policy' and 'operations' would meet. The arrangement seemed to work well for a time, but like much else it was soon overtaken by other developments and reorganizations. I thought it ironic, and misguided, when the separation of policy from operations later came to be seen as a necessary principle of good public administration.

An Independent Inspectorate of Prisons

The appointment of an independent Chief Inspector of Prisons became the most significant and long-lasting outcome of the May Committee's review. The committee had said in their report that

> ...we have no doubt both that the prison service would benefit from and that public sentiment requires that as many aspects of government...should be opened up to as wide an audience as possible. We therefore think that there should be a system of inspection of the prison service which although not "independent" of...the Home Office...should nevertheless be distanced from it as far as may be practicable.

There was already a chief inspector of prisons, a position established as a result of the Mountbatten review, but the chief inspector was part of the management of the Prison Department, a member of the Prisons Board, bound by the policies of ministers and subject to the constraints on the department's resources. From the Prison Department's point of view an independent inspectorate would on the one hand create a new and potentially troublesome source of interference and criticism; on the other, an authoritative, respected and independent inspectorate might have an influence on political and public opinion in ways which were helpful to the service in dealing with its problems of capacity and overcrowding. Taking that and the broader considerations of accountability and transparency into account, the Home Secretary accepted the committee's recommendation

and announced[4] that a chief inspector would be appointed, independent of the
Home Office, with terms of reference

To inspect and report to the Secretary of State on prison service establishments
in England and Wales, and, in particular, on
   (a)   conditions in those establishments;
   (b)   the treatment of prisoners and other inmates and the facilities available
         to them;
   (c)   such other matters as the Secretary of State may direct.

The statement added that the chief inspector would submit an annual
report which would be published, and other reports which would be made
publicly available as appropriate.

The terms of reference having been announced, we still had to convert
the May Committee's rather vague recommendation into an understanding
about the chief inspector's relationship with the Prison Department and
with prison establishments and their boards of visitors. In consultation with
colleagues, I drew up a 'charter' which said that the inspectorate's main occu-
pation would be the regular inspections of establishments, concentrating on
such as matters as the morale of staff and prisoners; the quality of the regime;
the condition of the buildings; questions of humanity and decency; and
whether the establishment was giving value for money.[5] Inspectors would not
be concerned with matters of administrative detail or investigate individual
grievances on the part of staff or inmates, but they would draw attention to
any general pattern of complaint if it seemed to point to some inadequacy
in management. Reports would be submitted to the Home Secretary with
a presumption that they would be published in the form in which they had
been submitted; the chief inspector might consult the Prison Department to
check matters of fact but would not offer drafts for comment and he or she
would have complete independence in determining the form and content
of their reports. Other paragraphs dealt with the process for drawing up

4.   *Hansard,* 30 April 1980, col 1395.
5.   The Charter was published as an annex to the Chief Inspector's first annual report — Home
     Office *Report of Her Majesty's Chief of Prisons for England and Wales 1981,* Cmnd 8532, London:
     HMSO, 1982.

the inspection programme, the investigation of incidents, the conduct of inspections and investigations, correspondence with prisoners and Members of Parliament, liaison with the Prison Department and the inspectorate's relationship with boards of visitors.

Essential features were the combination of the inspectorate's independence and its focus on 'humanity and decency' for prisoners and for members and staff. Its purpose was to be neither a pressure group working on behalf of prisoners, nor an instrument for carrying out government policy or increasing efficiency. The charter was later overtaken by the inspectorate's own statements of its methods and the criteria it would use, but it established a relationship which has been successfully continued since that time. The chief inspector's independence and authority were later emphasised when the office was placed on a statutory footing, with the title 'Her Majesty's Chief Inspector of Prisons' , in the Criminal Justice Act 1982.

The next issue was the appointment of the first chief inspector. Open advertisements and competitions for such a post were almost unknown at that time: it was taken for granted that a suitable person would be identified and invited to accept the post. Within the Home Office, it was argued that no one from the criminal justice services themselves would have sufficient independence or credibility; a judge or lawyer would adopt too legalistic an approach; a member of the armed forces would have too militaristic an attitude to prison staff and prison management; and so on. Bill Pearce, the chief probation officer for Inner London, was offered and accepted the post but sadly became ill and died soon afterwards. Later appointments — a prison governor in an acting capacity (Bill Brister), a diplomat (Sir James Hennessey), judge (Sir Stephen Tumim), a general (Sir David, now Lord, Ramsbotham) and a human rights lawyer (Anne Owers) — showed that assumptions should never be made on a basis of professional (or any other) stereotypes.

Director of Operational Policy 1980-1982

I was subsequently appointed to the new post of Director of Operational Policy which I had designed, although not intentionally for myself, and to the Prisons Board. As well as the other members of the Prisons Board, my immediate colleagues included Gordon Lakes and Brian Emes among the former governors, and Joe Pilling and then Quentin Thomas among the administrators.

The Prison Service at that time was in a constant state of crisis, whether from unrest among prisoners, escapes, assaults on prisoners, industrial action by prison officers or simply overcrowding. There had recently been riots at Gartree and Wormwood Scrubs Prisons and the service was still recovering from them. The demands for greater security in the 'dispersal' or 'Category A' prisons always seemed to take absolute priority and in prisons as elsewhere it became impossible to question the need for some new process or device, or its affordability, once it was known to be available.

It was the time when Dennis Trevelyan described prison conditions as 'an affront to civilised society', and John McCarthy resigned as governor of Wormwood Scrubs after writing a letter to *The Times* in which he said his prison felt like a 'large penal dustbin'. The dispute with the POA was still unresolved and prison officers' refusal to admit prisoners to ordinary prisons which were technically overcrowded led to the opening of two temporary prisons staffed by members of the armed forces, including the Royal Military Police where direct contact with prisoners was involved. Penal reformers have often presented overcrowding as the main problem which the service had to face. They defined it as the difference between a prison's 'certified normal accommodation' or CNA (essentially, its number of cells, with an assumption that cells should have no more than one occupant) and the actual number of prisoners at any one time. That number might be very much greater, with many prisoners being 'doubled up' or 'trebled up' (it was only recently that 'doubling' had been permitted—it had previously been forbidden in the belief that it might encourage homosexuality). Many people thought that for prisoners to share a cell, as in the television series *Porridge*, was a not serious hardship and even an advantage because they would have company during the long periods they would spend there.

The problem about which Trevelyan and McCarthy complained was not simply one of overcrowding in that sense, but also the associated problems of lack of access to night sanitation (hence 'slopping out'), the limited time which prisoners could spend out of their cells, and the lack of constructive activity, whether it was work or education. Shortages of staff combined with difficult industrial relations could interfere with visits and cause workshops to be closed or classes to be cancelled. 'Overcrowding drafts' to less crowded prisons could result in prisoners being moved to distant prisons with little or no notice, either for themselves or their families. The situation for young offenders and for women and girls had deteriorated markedly over the previous six years. Establishments for young offenders no longer received the special attention they had once enjoyed, and a combination of operational demands (or sometimes institutional convenience) and pressure on resources had made borstals almost indistinguishable from men's prisons. The women's system was struggling with the disruption caused by the rebuilding of Holloway and the shortcomings of the design (see *Chapter 3*), and the prison was beset by operational problems and difficult relations with the staff. In the circumstances of the time I felt unable to do much about either of those situations.

All those factors contributed to the precarious situation to which I return in the next chapter. I set out my view of the situation, and of the way in which I thought it might develop in the future, in a talk to a boards of visitors' conference, later published in *Prison Service Journal*.[6]

The Service's Identity and Purpose

There was much concern about the 'unity' of the service, and the need for a 'mission statement'[7]. I argued that the service should not be seen as consisting only of governors and prison officers (as the POA would have liked), and for a more inclusive identity in which its other members—administrative staff, instructors, medical staff—could feel they were equally valued; and resisted proposals for militarisation, for example uniforms and badges of rank for governors or giving the principal of the staff college the title 'commandant'. I was unable to prevent a change from plain clothes to uniforms for prison officers in borstals: the Prison Board justified its decision to make the change as being in the interests of 'the unity of the service', but it was mainly to avoid a dispute with the POA about the clothing allowance for officers wearing plain clothes. The board successfully resisted arguments that

---

6.   'Text of an address to the S W Region Board of Visitors Conference in July 1982', *Prison Service Journal*, October 1982, 18-20.

7.   It later emerged as 'Her Majesty's Prison Service serves the public by keeping in custody those committed by the courts. Our duty is to look after them with humanity and help them lead law-abiding and useful lives in custody and after release.'

the overcrowding crisis demanded the closure of Grendon as a specialised, psychiatrically supported prison so that the buildings could be used as an ordinary, overcrowded, secure prison providing another 200 places.

The service, and especially the Prisons Board, was also engaged in some serious self-questioning about the its identity and purpose. Its character and culture were still evolving to come to terms with the effects of the Mountbatten report. For prison officers the 'place to be' was no longer on landings working with prisoners and getting to know prisoners but in control rooms or with dog sections. More successful careers were to be made in developing new forms of security and the technology to support it, and in applying them to the structure of buildings and the management of institutions. Even though the Prisons Board and most governors no longer believed that they could 'cure' offending behaviour, or successfully train people to live a 'good and useful life after release' (in the words of the Prison Rules), they still wanted to do more than run prisons that were safe and secure. They realised that to do that the service needed to treat prisoners with humanity and decency, and it needed a vision and a sense of direction that was more than the bleak vision of 'positive custody', put forward by the May Committee, or the more progressive 'humane containment' which Roy King and Rod Morgan had proposed.[8]

The board had useful but inconclusive discussions which covered such subjects as the ethos of the service and a discipline of 'accountable regimes' and 'minimum standards', later picked up by the Woolf report's recommendation for 'accredited standards'. The hope at the time was that if pressures of overcrowding made it impossible for the Prison Service to meet those standards, the courts would be willing to adjust their sentences accordingly. That was always unrealistic, but the concept of standards was later developed by successive chief inspectors of prisons. Both could in some ways be seen as examples of what later came to be known as the 'new public management', although without the emphasis on competition and centralised micro-management that came to be associated with it.

I tried to alert colleagues to the more immediate and pressing issues of racial discrimination which prison psychologists had begun to uncover in some establishments, and to lay the foundations of a policy for dealing with

8.   Roy King and Rod Morgan *The Future of the Prison System*, London: Gower, 1980.

them. I was pleased to find that boards of visitors were becoming more assertive, and I welcomed the formation of an independent Association of Members of Boards of Visitors which would not be effectively under Prison Service control.

The 'Justice Model'

I also argued for what I called a 'justice model', emphasising certainty, propriety and standards of conduct and physical accommodation which would combine the best elements of the rehabilitation or treatment models and I hoped give the service a stronger identity and sense of purpose. The idea revived and built on the issues of procedural justice and legitimacy that I had raised eight years before. I noticed the way in which the Royal Military Police had dealt with prisoners at the emergency camps, including simple things like calling them by their names and saying 'please' and 'thank you', but there were wider issues about, for example, the possessions they were allowed to have with them in their cells and the responsibility they were expected to take and the choices they were allowed. Quentin Thomas wrote a detailed paper which we put to the Prisons Board in which he argued:

> Under the justice model the only aim of imprisonment, indeed its only justification, is that it is a punishment that is appropriate, on a judicial assessment of just deserts to the offence. But the punishment derives entirely from the imprisonment—the deprivation of liberty—and not from the conditions of the incarceration …

> The justice model applied to internal prison management implies minimum standards governing conditions; the enhancement of rights and the duty of care to the greatest extent compatible with closed prison security; providing the resources and machinery to activate such rights; the acceptance of humane containment, in its fullest sense, as the main goal of the system, rather than corrective treatment or moral improvement as ends in themselves; and to enhance "activities" for work, education and leisure as close as possible to what is available in the outside society.

> The counter-argument that such a regime would "lack moral purpose" is a misconception. The model may be seen as envisaging a clear moral purpose, though

one different from that articulated at the heyday of the treatment model. The aim would be to achieve—as an over-riding and public objective—fairness and justice in all the everyday details of officer behaviour towards inmates. The Justice model thus becomes a rallying point for self respect for staff, the standard by which its professionalism may be measured, a source of clear guidance and a principle that inmates can certainly understand and (conceivably) respect.

This need not involve a greater resort to court enforcement of such rights, but a framework to ensure their activation and enforcement is sorely needed now and would be equally urgent under the justice model aegis.

I explained what we had in mind in a talk at the Prison Governors' Conference in 1982, when I said:

The justice model, with its emphasis on certainty, propriety and standards of conduct and physical accommodation, offers the ingredients of a new approach which, combined with the best elements of the rehabilitative or treatment model, could give the Prison Service a revived professional identity and sense of purpose. Some of the principles might be

- A reaffirmation that offenders should be sent to prison as a punishment and not for punishment. Patterson's dictum has become a cliché and is largely disregarded by staff.
- Recognition that staff and prisoners are equal as human beings and equal before the law.
- Attention to the dictum of Lord Wilberforce that 'Under English law, a convicted prisoner, in spite of his imprisonment, retains all civil rights which are not expressly taken away or by necessary implication.'
- Recognition that the purpose of a prison sentence, and the purpose of the Prison Service in giving effect to it, is to deprive the offender of his liberty for the period which the court has judged necessary to mark the gravity of his offence—and no more than that.
- What is meant by deprivation of liberty for this purpose should be spelt out explicitly in Prison Rules.
- Recognition that the Secretary of State, acting through the Prison Service, has an obligation to provide the prisoner with decent living conditions

and with opportunities to occupy himself, to keep in touch with his family and friends, within reason to develop his abilities and personality, to look after his health, to follow his religion, and to prepare for his release. Appropriate machinery for these obligations to be enforced.

- The highest standards of equity and propriety in all dealings between staff and prisoners.
- Ultimate accountability to the courts in matters of the prisoner's facilities, treatment and conditions.

The justice model made little progress at the time, but some of its ideas later formed the basis for the sentencing provisions of the Criminal Justice Act 1991 (see *Chapter 8*) and were reflected in Lord Justice Woolf's report on the disturbances in 1990 and his recommendations for 'justice in prisons.' They were later developed into the principles of 'decency' and the 'healthy prison' promoted by Richard Tilt and Martin Narey as Directors General, by David Ramsbotham and Anne Owers as HM Chief Inspectors, and by Tony Bottoms and Tom Tyler in their work on legitimacy.[9],[10]

I left the Prison Department in the autumn of 1982. Difficult times continued, with a long running struggle for power between management and the Prison Officers' Association, periodical disturbances culminating in those at Manchester and other prisons in April 1990, and further pressures on the prison population. To those were later added the department's transition to an executive agency and the contracting-out of prisons and prison functions which I discuss in *Chapter 10*.

The prison population at the beginning of the 1980s was still about 40,000 but it was now growing rapidly.

---

9.   Richard Sparks, Anthony Bottoms and Will Hay, *Prisons and the Problem of Order*, Oxford University Press, 1996. Tom Tyler *Why People Obey the Law: Procedural Justice, Legitimacy and Compliance*, Princeton University Press, 2006.

10. Barbara Hudson and others subsequently criticised the 'justice model' as being associated with rigid and severe sentencing and repressive aims in the treatment of offenders, in the United Kingdom and the United States. That version of the model was very different from the approach which we were proposing in the early-1980s. Barbara Hudson *Justice through Punishment: A Critique of the 'Justice' Model of Corrections*, London: Palgrave Macmillan, 1987.

CHAPTER 5

New Approaches to Crime and Justice

I expected, and would have been happy, to stay at the Prison Department for another three or four years, but in September 1982 I was to my surprise promoted to Deputy Secretary to take charge of the Criminal and Statistical Departments and the Home Office Research Unit. It was the job I had always coveted, and I had the good fortune to stay in it for eight years.

The Context

The change of government in 1979, and Sir Brian Cubbon's appointment as Permanent Secretary at about the same time, brought a change of culture to the Home Office, or at least to its senior management. Some senior posts were abolished, including the deputy secretary (grade 2) level post of Chief Scientist. Any new work had to be done by existing staff and within existing structures and budgets. There were to be no special teams or task forces and no major changes in organization. The department's job was no longer to be seen as managing a process, but as achieving an outcome or a result. The change was one which I personally welcomed and was glad to support.

The national context included the Thatcher government's Financial Management Initiative (FMI), with its emphasis on efficiency, economy and effectiveness which I had no problem in accepting, and its social policies and attitudes with which I had more difficulty. Fortunately from my point of view they did not have much immediate impact on the Home Office, and we did not have to be committed to them ourselves. The ministers with whom I had most contact came from an older and more generous tradition of Conservatism, which Douglas Hurd celebrated in his speech in Tamworth to mark the bicentenary of Robert Peel's birth in 1788. We were fortunate that throughout the 1980s there was a broad consensus in support of the things we were trying to do, between all the main political parties, with the main resistance coming from within the Conservative party itself. We were well aware of the government's political position and the constraints it placed on us, but the Prime Minister's Office took surprisingly little interest in Home Office business except during the coalminers' strike in 1984. I do not remember any occasion when Mrs Thatcher intervened or commented on any matter within my own area of responsibility.[1]

The legislative landmarks of the period include the Criminal Justice Acts of 1982, 1987, 1988[2] and 1991, the Police and Criminal Evidence Act 1984, the Prosecution of Offences Act 1985 and the Public Order Act 1986. I was mainly concerned with the four Criminal Justice Acts, and especially the Criminal Justice Act 1991. But I would like to think that my main contribution was not so much in legislation or in administrative reorganization (of which there was very little during that period) as in trying to improve the dynamics and relationships involved in the criminal justice process; working towards a shared sense of direction; and so ultimately I hoped improving the quality of justice and reducing crime.

The Job I Had to Do

My main responsibilities included policy and legislation on criminal justice, probation and magistrates' courts (then and until 1992 a Home Office responsibility), together with research and statistics for the Home Office as a whole. I was not otherwise concerned with police, prisons, immigration or broadcasting. It was part of the culture of the Home Office that the different departments, and the divisions within them, did not interfere with each other's business but Brian Cubbon's weekly meetings of deputy secretaries brought a degree of corporate management which I thought worked well. Other deputy secretaries were Wilfred Hyde (Immigration and Broadcasting), Michael Moriarty (Principal Establishment Officer), James Nursaw (Legal Adviser), Michael Partridge and then John Chilcot (Police), and Dennis Trevelyan, succeeded by Chris Train (Prisons). On my own side of the office my immediate colleagues included Bill Bohan, later succeeded by Graham

1.   Stephen Farrall and Colin Hay have speculated on the reasons for which the government was not more aggressively radical during the period of Margaret Thatcher's administration. They suggest that they included her preoccupation with other subjects and the influence of other members of her government and her party. Stephen Farrall and Colin Hay 'Not So Tough on Crime? Why Weren't the Thatcher Governments More Radical in Reforming the Criminal Justice System?', *British Journal of Criminology* (2010), 50, 550-559.

2.   The Criminal Justice Acts 1987 and 1988 were essentially one Act, but became separated by the intervention of the general election in 1987.

Angel, Bill Jeffrey, Jean Goose and Bob Baxter (Criminal Policy Department); Michael Head (Criminal Justice and Constitutional Department); Philippa Drew (Probation Service Division); Rita Maurice and Chris Lewis (Statistical Department); and Ron Clarke, Mary Tuck, John Graham, Mike Hough, Tim Newburn and later Chris Nuttall[3] (Research Unit).

William Whitelaw was succeeded as Home Secretary by Leon Brittan (later Lord Brittan of Spennithorne) in 1983 and then by Douglas Hurd in 1985. I worked closely and I think successfully with David Mellor and later with John Patten (now Lord Patten) as ministers of state, and I had good relations with successive political advisers, especially Douglas Hurd's adviser Edward Bickham. He and I established a clear understanding about what our respective jobs were and the relationship between them. His was to help the minister in his relations and to promote his interests with Parliament and his political party; mine was to advise on policy and to bring it into effect. We were able to work successfully together, for example when he was helping to draft the Conservative party's manifesto for the 1987 election (see *Chapter 9*), with no sense of rivalry or opposition and with common aims and shared objectives where the substantive issues were concerned.

My job was set out in a 'charter' which I drafted myself and agreed with the Permanent Secretary. It was essentially to reduce crime, improve the quality of justice, achieve a better system of operational and financial management in the probation and magistrates' courts' services, improve cooperation between government departments and between the criminal justice services, and coordinate the government's response to crime across Whitehall. It included recognising the interdependence as well as the independence of the different criminal justice services, improving cooperation between them, and the relatively new concept of 'managing the criminal justice system' (see *Chapter 6*). I was also to promote the contribution of research and statistics to the formation and evaluation of policy, to look after (I could hardly say 'manage') the department's relationships with the higher judiciary, and to be on terms with leading academics and (remarkably as it might now seem) newspaper columnists.

Experience had already taught me that progress is more likely to be made,

3. Chris Nuttall was later appointed to succeed Rita Maurice as Director for both research and statistics.

and to be sustainable, if it is the outcome of discussion, understanding and agreement, and if it is 'owned' by those directly involved, than if it is imposed by central direction, organizational change or legislation. Those may sometimes be needed but they should if possible give effect to a change that has already been agreed or at least accepted. They are not ends in themselves, and unless their purpose is simply to give an impression of government activity, their only value is in the practical results they produce. It is better for services themselves to develop and 'own' good practice as part of their own professionalism, than to follow it because it is what government tells them to do. Results depend on the relationships and dynamics among the people directly involved. That was the approach which I tried to follow, for example in applying the government's Financial Management Initiative both within the Home Office itself and to the probation and magistrates' courts' services.

I became convinced of the importance of lateral communications and 'horizontal vision', and of the need to improve them — across government, with and between the services, within the Home Office itself. There were already clear signs that the new emphasis on accountable management and narrowly defined objectives could discourage cooperation with others who had different objectives of their own, and could make it more difficult to deal with the complex situations that are characteristic of criminal justice and attempts to reduce crime. The problem of 'silos' later came to be recognised as one which affected government as a whole, as it still does.

The Policy-making Process

The shaping of policy towards criminal justice during most of the period since the Criminal Justice Act 1948 had been described as haphazard and as pragmatic and reactive.[4] During the 1970s the Home Office had begun to move towards a more strategic view of criminal justice, with the formation of the Crime Policy Planning Unit in 1974 and the publication of *A Review*

---

4. Michael Moriarty, 'The Policy-Making Process: how it is seen from the Home Office', in *Policy-Making in England,* edited by Nigel Walker, Cambridge: Institute for Criminology, 1977, page 134. Also Anthony Bottoms and Simon Stevenson, 'What Went Wrong? Criminal Justice Policy in England and Wales, 1945-1970', in *Unravelling Criminal Justice: Eleven British Studies,* edited by David Downes, London: Macmillan, 1992.

of Criminal Justice Policy 1976[5] which focused mainly on the prison population, the use of custodial and non-custodial sentences, and communications with the judiciary. Ministers and officials still saw an offender's punishment as being the sentence of the court and the loss of liberty, time, money or choice which followed from the sentence. It was not for the prison or probation services to add to that punishment by deliberately making conditions or requirements more painful or humiliating than was necessary for the proper management of the institution or programme of supervision, although that 'necessity' might be interpreted in more or less restrictive ways.

Chapter 1 described how much of the process of policy making had traditionally been informed by reports from expert advisory bodies. The Conservative government now regarded the members of such bodies as out of touch, self-interested or politically prejudiced: no more were set up for some time, the Advisory Council on the Penal System was abolished and the Criminal Law Revision Committee ceased to function. Their loss left a void in policy-making which we had to try to fill ourselves. That involved extending our own knowledge, contacts and understanding in ways that were not familiar to us.

With ministers' and Brian Cubbon's encouragement, I saw it as part of my colleagues' and my own job to look for and listen to new ideas, to talk about them with anyone—academics, practitioners, voluntary organizations—who might be interested and have something to contribute, to explore their implications and their feasibility, and then to refine and develop them into suggestions or proposals which we could put to ministers.[6] Discussion could be free and open up to that point, provided that it was not used to prejudice

---

5. Home Office, *A Review of Criminal Justice Policy 1976*, London: HMSO, 1977, written by Michael Moriarty.
6. Lord Windlesham described the characteristic contribution of the senior civil servant '[as lying] not so much in the originality and imagination he or she may display in thinking up policies—these can be a positive nuisance without the ability to convince and lead those, often outside the service, who will have to put them into effect—but the skills to recognise promising new ideas and the opportunities to develop them, and to exploit the opportunities when they occur...
    The process of fusing ministerial intentions and departmental expertise in the formulation of policy is a great deal more subtle than it appears at first sight. Proposals seldom spring from a single source...'
    Lord Windlesham, *Responses to Crime*, Vol 2, *Penal Policy in the Making*, Oxford: Clarendon Press, 1993, pages 13-14.

a decision which had still to be taken or to undermine a decision once it had been made. I hoped that consultation would in that way become a continuous dialogue, not confined to formal processes or specific consultation exercises. A useful feature was the two 'working papers'[7] which did not announce any new policies or initiatives but set out to explain what the government was doing so that it would be better understood and we could try to establish the sense of a shared, non-political, public purpose.

Voluntary organizations such as the National Association for the Care and Rehabilitation of Offenders (NACRO, later Nacro), with Vivien (now Baroness) Stern as its director, also promoted their own practical schemes for reducing crime and the resettlement of offenders, and those together with their own research—for example Nacro's work on the treatment of ethnic minorities—proved valuable and influential. Paul Cavadino, the secretary of the Parliamentary All-Party Penal Affairs Group and based at Nacro, was always a master of the facts and of the latest developments and their implications. He was an invaluable source of information and advice for Parliament, journalists and the Home Office itself. Few specific proposals or initiatives originated directly from ministers or their political advisers; exceptions were the new voluntary organization to prevent and reduce crime, and the Victim's Charter—see *Chapter 8*.

To mark the bicentenary of the Home Office in 1982, Brian Cubbon arranged a series of lectures and discussions which were later published as *The Home Office: Perspectives on Policy and Administration*.[8] The speakers were James Callaghan, former Home Secretary; Lord Allen of Abbeydale, former Permanent Secretary; Sir Cyril Phillips,[9] Professor Michael Zander; Lord Windlesham; and Hugo Young, then joint deputy editor of the *Sunday Times*. Participants included past and present ministers and civil servants, journalists and academics. Some of the lectures dealt mainly with specific aspects of Home Office business, others with the character of the Home

---

7.   Home Office, *Criminal Justice: A Working Paper*, London: Home Office, 1984, revised (and much improved) edition 1986.
8.   *The Home Office: Perspectives on Policy and Administration*, London: Royal Institute for Public Administration, 1983.
9.   Sir Cyril Phillips had chaired the Royal Commission on Criminal Procedure whose report led to the Police and Criminal Evidence Act 1984 and the formation of the Crown Prosecution Service—see *Chapter 6*.

Office as a whole. Perhaps the most penetrating and critical was Hugo Young's lecture on 'The Department of Civil Liberties', where he drew attention to the paradox that the department which claimed to be, and probably was, the country's main guardian of civil liberties within government also exercised the powers and functions which were the greatest threat to them. He argued for the European Convention on Human Rights to be incorporated into domestic law so that issues of human rights, including prisoners' rights, could be settled in the domestic courts without having to be referred to the European Court of Human Rights in Strasbourg; and also for the creation of a Ministry of Justice separate from the Home Office. They were radical and controversial proposals at the time; both were adopted later but the controversy continues—see *Chapter 10*.

Brian Cubbon also convened a series of internal seminars, followed by a weekend meeting with ministers, to establish a strategy for the department's approach to crime and the means of preventing and responding to it. The aim was to review the research and the policy options, and to take a long term view and set a sense of direction that would extend to the end of the Parliament and beyond. He was conscious, as I had been during my time at the Cabinet Office, that the Home Office was not especially well-regarded in other parts of Whitehall, and while other permanent secretaries could point to the tangible improvements which their departments were making in hospitals, schools, housing or road building (not all of which appeared so successful in retrospect), the Home Office had less to show for itself, and seemed to be constantly in crisis and to be having little impact on crime.

The principal conclusion from my point of view was that the country could not rely on the criminal justice system to prevent or reduce crime, and it had to look to wider social and environmental policies to prevent and reduce crime (see *Chapter 8*). It was just as important to improve the quality of justice as it affected not only defendants and offenders but also victims and the country as a whole, and we had to recognise that fear of crime and public confidence were now emerging as issues in their own right. We began to learn the discipline of including numbers in our proposals and submissions—timescales, costs, inputs and outputs—although we were cautious about promising outcomes in terms such as rates of reoffending or levels of crime which depended on factors which we could neither predict nor control. Unquantified arguments about quality, equity or fairness became harder to sustain, although the underlying and mostly unspoken values were broadly understood.

James Callaghan had suggested in his bicentenary lecture that the Home Office should have a responsibility for assembling a broad overall view of the interaction of government measures and policies on the development of society. Some questioned that suggestion in the discussion which followed. There seemed to be fairly general agreement about the limitations on what the Home Office and the criminal justice system could themselves do to prevent or reduce crime, but if a role of that kind was needed it might be better placed in the Cabinet Office, for example, than in the Home Office where the issues might too often come to be seen from a perspective of crime and criminal justice, with criminal law and law enforcement as the solution.[10] Wherever the responsibility was placed, success would depend on a collective commitment on the part of government as a whole. That seemed unlikely at that time, although no one was impolite enough to say so.

Research and Statistics

The Home Office Research Unit had a special and sometimes controversial place in the culture and structure of the department. Under Tom Lodge and John Croft as successive heads of the unit, it had by the early 1980s built up a strong reputation in the academic community, both in the United Kingdom and abroad. John Croft retired in 1983, to be followed first by Ron Clarke and then by Mary Tuck in 1985. The unit was having an increasing influence both on policy and professional practice, but in political circles it was gaining a reputation for 'liberal' thought and a sense that it was beginning to have an identity and approach of its own, separate from those of ministers. Under the Conservative government, the Financial Management Initiative and the government's emphasis on information, evaluation and results gave the unit a powerful influence on the formation of policy, but it was also under greater pressure to demonstrate that it was giving value for money and had to avoid any suggestion that the unit was in any way questioning the government's own policies or political direction. A separate, older and

---

10. As happened with drugs—see *Chapter 8*.

larger, Statistical Department was responsible for maintaining the Criminal, Prison, Immigration and other statistics, with Rita Maurice as its director.

Several strands of research, both by the Home Office Research Unit and in universities and research institutes, were especially relevant. Some of them had produced negative results. They included the lack of evidence that either severity in sentencing or the number of police officers patrolling the streets had any significant effect on the general level of crime, although the visible presence of police officers was important for public confidence.[11] Both of those findings seemed contrary to common sense and the findings were contested and widely disbelieved, as they still are today, but no new evidence has emerged which seriously challenges them. We felt that we had to accept the lack of evidence that prison regimes or probation programmes had much effect on reoffending, but we were reluctant to accept the bleak conclusion which had been taken from Robert Martinson's widely quoted but sometimes misunderstood study showing that 'nothing works'.[12] We were clear that no one should ever be sent prison because it would 'do them good' (as had sometimes been argued for borstal training), but we believed and wanted to show that at least some things can work, with some people, some of the time.

There was increasing and encouraging evidence, from Great Britain and the United States, that physical and 'situational' measures can have a significant impact on levels of crime if they are well-designed and targeted—not only improvements in physical security but also in the design and management of housing estates, keeping buildings and public spaces in good repair, and engaging local communities.[13] Its application is described in *Chapter 8*. Work by David Farrington and others showed the correlation between criminal behaviour and a person's domestic, social and economic circumstances and how criminal behaviour can often extend from generation to generation. Disturbing evidence was emerging of both direct and indirect racial discrimination, at almost every stage of the criminal justice process and in

---

11. Stephen Brody, *The Effectiveness of Sentencing*, Home Office Research Study No 35, London: Home Office, 1975. Ron Clarke and Mike Hough, *Crime and Police Effectiveness*, London: Home Office Research Unit, 1984.
12. Robert Martinson 'What Works? Questions and Answers about Penal Reform', *Public Interest*, Spring 1974, 35, pp 22-57.
13. Ron Clarke and Pat Mayhew (eds.), *Designing Out Crime*, London: HMSO, 1980.

the criminal justice services themselves—again, see *Chapter 8*. Research by David Smith, Robert Reiner, Rod Morgan and others at the Policy Studies Institute was producing important and sometimes disturbing insights into the nature of police accountability and the dynamics of policing as it was carried out on the ground.

An important innovation was the British Crime Survey (now the Crime Survey for England and Wales), approved rather nervously by ministers who thought—rightly—that it would show that actual levels of crime as experienced by its victims were higher than those of crimes recorded by the police and published in the Criminal Statistics. Their fear that the results would add to public alarm seems not to have been realised, although fear of crime and demands for action were increasing as more people (and especially more middle-class people) suffered from it. Researchers hoped that the survey would show that crime, especially burglary, was not rising as fast as the Criminal Statistics indicated, and that at least part of the increase was because more crimes were being reported and recorded, but that hope was largely disappointed.

An unexpected result of the survey was the realisation that only a very small proportion of the crimes experienced by victims is followed by a conviction and sentence. That confirmed the view of researchers and officials that the criminal justice process had only a limited impact on the general level of crime, but it may have added to a decline in public confidence and to public impatience with the system as a whole. Also significant was the—for most people surprising—discovery that about 30 per cent of the male population had a conviction for a 'standard list' offence by the time they were 30, confirming that 'criminals' should not be thought of as a separate class of people, different from the 'normal' part of the population or people 'like ourselves'.

We tried to make the presentation of research and statistics more accessible and interesting and their results more widely known. We introduced a periodical *Digest of Information on the Criminal Justice System in England and Wales* which brought together the relevant data from various sources in a single document which was readily available to managers and practitioners, and to teachers and students in training schools, colleges and universities. We held meetings between the Research Unit's own researchers and those in universities to help plan the unit's future programme of funding and in-house research, taking a strategic view over a longer term than the usual political horizon. We introduced a practice, led by Rita Maurice, of regularly reviewing the latest statistics and projections and their implications for policy.

There was always an underlying concern about the publication of research which might be inconvenient for ministers. The rule was that we should never give way to self-censorship, but we should make sure that the quality of the research and its presentation could withstand rigorous and sometimes hostile criticism. Mary Tuck once said it was the job of the Research Unit to 'speak truth to power'; I added 'in a voice to which it would listen'. I remember only one occasion when the publication of a research report—on the effectiveness of policing—was seriously challenged, and that was not by ministers but by colleagues within the department who questioned whether the conclusions in the original draft were adequately supported by the evidence. The draft was amended and the report was eventually published. Ministers occasionally questioned whether a research study had any practical value and its significance and value then had to be carefully explained, but I can remember no occasion when a report was altered at their instigation or its publication significantly delayed. Ministerial sensitivities did not at that time require a disclaimer saying that the report did not necessarily represent the views of the government.

We made a serious attempt to take academic thought, research and statistics into account in the formulation of policy both at a strategic level and in the development of practice. Policy was evidence-based in that broad sense, and research was especially influential in areas such as the deterrent effect of sentencing, the effectiveness of penal treatment, the means of preventing and reducing crime and the impact of the criminal justice process on members of minority groups. There was a common understanding about the kinds of things that could or needed to be done, brought together in the Home Office Research Unit and previously reflected in the reports of the Advisory Council on the Penal System, and to varying degrees shared by others in Europe, the Commonwealth and the United States. In England, it came to be portrayed as an understanding shared only by an exclusive elite, and it did not survive the political pressures and the social changes of the period, especially after 1992.[14]

---

14. For a further discussion of research and scientific advice in government, see *Where Next for Criminal Justice?*, pages 180-181.

Relations with the Judiciary

There had for some years been concern about the lack of communication between the Home Office and the judiciary. Judges and magistrates were encouraged to visit prisons but judges rarely did so. During the 1960s, judges had begun to hold periodical meetings at which Home Office officials, including prison governors and sometimes myself, would explain what happened to a person after they received a prison or borstal sentence, and in time they grew into residential seminars which included exercises in sentencing under the auspices of the Judicial Studies Board. The Home Office also produced a booklet *The Sentence of the Court,* mainly for magistrates. It was not clear whether they had any effect, and booklet was sometimes resented as improper interference. To their proper insistence on keeping their independence was now added the judges' concern that any attempt to bring about a closer relationship was prompted by an economically driven wish to influence sentencing and their use of imprisonment.

Prompted by the crisis of prison overcrowding and industrial relations in 1981, two buffet suppers were arranged where members of the Prisons Board described the situation in prisons and there was then an opportunity for discussion. They proved to be awkward occasions, for all concerned, and they were not repeated. A misunderstanding over the proposal for administrative early release, relations between the Home Office and the higher judiciary more or less broke down. Even so Lord Lane, Lord Chief Justice, was not unsympathetic, and in two judgements from the Court of Appeal (in the cases of *Upton* and *Bibi*[15]) he encouraged shorter sentences to take account of the situation in prisons.

Through the good offices of Sir Derek Oulton, the Permanent Secretary at the then Lord Chancellor's Department, it was arranged that I should have regular meetings with Lord Justice Tasker Watkins, the Senior Presiding Judge and later Deputy Lord Chief Justice, to exchange information and sometimes views on matters of concern to either of us. I sometimes went alone and sometimes with colleagues. After a tentative start, the meetings went well, usually dealing with relatively routine matters of procedure but sometimes with more substantive issues. One example was the judges' wish for a power for the Court of Appeal to increase as well as reduce sentences

---

15. *Upton* (1980) 71 Cr. App. R. 102 at 104; *Bibi* (1980) 71 Cr. App. R. 360 at 361.

in cases which came before it, provided by the provision in the Criminal Justice Act 1988 for the Attorney General to refer to it what might appear to be unduly lenient sentences. I was able to mention the proposals which ministers or officials had in mind for future legislation, and to gauge his reactions to them before they reached the stage of ministerial approval or formal consultation. More sensitive issues included Lord Justice Watkins' discovery of ministers' practice, of which neither he nor I had been aware, in setting aside the trial judge's recommended term in life sentence cases (see *Chapter 6*); and the early ventures into restorative justice where judges were concerned that they might prejudice the trial (see *Chapter 8*). After a time it again became possible for the Home Secretary (by this time Douglas Hurd) and the Lord Chief Justice to meet periodically in the Home Secretary's office, with Lord Justice Watkins and myself in attendance and an agenda which we had jointly prepared beforehand.

Other regular contacts were through my own or my colleagues' attendance at the Judicial Studies Board or its committees, and regular meetings with the Magistrates' Association. I visited courts and probation services, and accepted invitations to speak at judges' sentencing seminars and at conferences and meetings throughout England and Wales and sometimes in Scotland. Among judges I had particular contact with Lord Justice Glidewell as chairman of the Judicial Studies Board, and with Lord Justice Henry Brooke and Lord Justice Auld. Among magistrates I had regular meetings with Douglas Acres, Jane Gummer, John Hoskins, Enid Ralphs, Margaret Romanes and Rosemary Thomson. Justices' Clerks included Bryan Gibson, Tony Heath, Ian McKittrick and David Simpson.

Beyond Whitehall

Looking beyond Whitehall, and with the support of David Mellor and later John Patten as ministers of state, we tried to establish a better understanding between the Home Office and those who would now be called 'stakeholders' — practitioners in the operational services, judges and magistrates, voluntary organizations (becoming increasingly important although there were many fewer than there are today), and with other government departments, academics and journalists. We made frequent visits out of the office, sometimes jointly but often on our own. Especially during the period

of consultation leading up to the Criminal Justice 1991 (see *Chapter 9*), John
Patten held a series of meetings with Conservative Members of Parliament.

I went to troubled areas and 'difficult' housing estates to talk to residents
and local services on their own ground in London, Birmingham, Liverpool
and Sheffield.[16] I established contacts and cordial relations with scholars
such as Andrew Ashworth, Anthony Bottoms, David Downes, Roger Hood,
Rod Morgan, Paul Rock and David Thomas; with the directors of voluntary
organizations such as Frances Crook at the Howard League, Vivien Stern
at Nacro, and Stephen Shaw at the Prison Reform Trust; with Paul Sieghart
at JUSTICE and the film-maker and criminologist Roger Graef. I was on
terms with journalists such as Malcolm Dean, Frances Gibb, Melanie Phillips,
Trevor Phillips, Joshua Rozenberg, Mary-Ann Sieghart and Alan Travis.

I greatly appreciated my visits to Scotland and the opportunity see something of the Scottish system—procurators fiscal, with lessons for the Crown
Prosecution Service in England and Wales; the system of non-adversarial
children's hearings; and the absence of a separate probation service. I liked
the small size of the system and the different dynamics which resulted from
it. I wondered whether it would ever be possible to reproduce some of its
features in a regional system south of the border, but that was never a practical possibility without a system of regional government.

I described the issues as we saw them in the Home Office, what we were
doing and the options we were considering, but also and just as important listened to what people were saying, responded positively if possible. I
emphasised the value of lateral vision and communication, sharing ideas and
information and working across organizational boundaries within government, with and between criminal justice services and the judiciary, and
between the criminal justice and other sectors. I explained the government's
and my own hopes and expectations. The talks I gave were essentially personal
statements of my own. The important point as I saw it, and which I think
the audiences appreciated, was that I was not making political speeches or
reflecting a political agenda, perhaps with a press release and a different and
more public audience in mind, but trying to engage in a serious discussion

---

16. Including in Sheffield the now famous (or infamous) Park Hill Estate, built with high hopes
      20 years before but where crime had now become a serious problem. Colin Thomas, the Chief
      Probation Officer, had recently opened a probation office on the estate itself.

on equal terms.

I did not ask colleagues to prepare drafts—they had enough to do without that, and what I wanted to say usually involved several parts of the Home Office and sometimes other government departments as well. I did however circulate the drafts quite widely and asked colleagues for comments. I kept ministers in touch, but I did not ask them to approve the drafts of my talks and there was never any suggestion that I should do so.

Beyond England and Wales

I made a several visits to other European countries and the United States. I visited troubled areas in cities such as Paris, Amsterdam, New York and Oakland, California. I learned a lot from the visits about ideas we might adopt in England and Wales—the coordination of services for young people in France and the distinctively French *politique de prevention*; the role played by younger, progressive judges in Germany; of prosecutors in The Netherlands and the Dutch scheme for weekend imprisonment; the functions of district attorneys in the United States and their relations with the police; and the practical work of the Vera Institute in New York and of the Centre for Court Innovation, then based in Denver and now in New York.

As a member of the United Nations Committee on Crime Prevention and Control I attended a number of the committee's meetings in Vienna, and I led the United Kingdom delegations to the United Nations Crime Congresses in Milan (1985) and Havana (1990). I was invited to become a member of the Advisory Board for the Helsinki Institute for Crime Prevention and Control, affiliated with the UN. I met a number of stimulating and distinguished colleagues, both in Helsinki and at the UN itself. I learned a good deal about the UN and its dynamics and politics, and I hope I made a useful contribution to its meetings, including an attempt to bring some discipline to the management of the UN Crime Programme, but I cannot say that its proceedings on crime or criminal justice ever had much influence in this country. I also travelled to New York to present the United Kingdom's five-yearly report to the United Nations Human Rights Committee on the International Covenant on Social and Political Rights—see *Chapter 11*. Some of my colleagues had a similar but probably more productive relationship with the Council of Europe, and members of the Research Unit had their own network of professional contacts in Europe, the Commonwealth and the United States. In all those contacts I felt that the United Kingdom had more in common with other countries in Northern Europe and the Commonwealth that with other parts of the world including the United States — as a society, in our attitudes and responses to crime, and in our arrangements for government if not in our legal system.

It was at that time the practice for an American scholar from the Vera Institute of Justice in New York to spend a period of time, typically about two years, as an observer with the Inner London Probation Service. Floyd Feeney was one of those who did so, followed by Chris Stone, now professors at the Universities of California and Harvard respectively. Their different backgrounds and lack of identification with any established interest in this country enabled them to gain a unique insight into what was happening on the ground and how people were thinking and feeling, and their impressions were especially valuable to us.

Informal Discussion Group

During the period when I was in the Prison Department I had established an informal discussion group, meeting on neutral territory, as a place where civil servants, practitioners, academics and people from voluntary organizations could discuss the issues of the moment as they saw them. The group met over a period of almost ten years, with changes of focus and membership to reflect changes in my own and other members' interests and responsibilities. I invited some Home Office colleagues to join the group; one or two preferred not to take part in that kind of debate, but most agreed and contributed freely to the discussion.

Vivien Stern hosted the meetings at what is now Nacro; other members of the group included at various times Andrew Ashworth, Anthony Bottoms, David Downes, Roger Hood, Roy King, Rod Morgan and Andrew Rutherford; and among my Home Office colleagues Bill Bohan, Margaret Clayton, Philippa Drew, Ian Dunbar, Tim Flesher, Arthur de Frisching, Cedric Fullwood, Jenny Hughes, Bill Jeffrey and Mary Tuck.

The group provided a 'quiet room' or a 'safe space' where it was possible to share ideas and impressions with people who were like-minded enough to find some ground but who had different backgrounds, perceptions and professional interests. We could speak or stay silent as we chose. There were no institutional positions that had to be defended, and no pressure to reach conclusions or outcomes. It was an opportunity to stop and ask 'Where will that take us? What effect will it have? Should we find out more, or do more research? Roy King [17] described the meetings as being

'... confidential in the sense that no-one would have wished to embarrass another member of the group by repeating things better not said in public, but if the discussion stimulated ideas for an article or for an initiative within the Prison Department, so much the better... Virtually no subject was excluded from the agenda of the meetings, and as the members of the group developed understanding and mutual respect so there was an unprecedented sharing of data and ideas, with opinions vigorously and freely expressed.'

Much of the discussion related to questions affecting prisons (while I was still at the Prison Department), and then to criminal law and sentencing and to the underlying principles and their implications. We explored a range of ideas and possibilities as events took their course, including the 'justice model' for imprisonment, the anomalies in sentencing and Andrew Ashworth's proposals for a Sentencing Council, David Downes' impressions of sentencing practice in The Netherlands, and the practicability of day or weekend imprisonment and day or unit fines. I also tried out my idea for an institute of justice (see *Chapter 10*). It is hard to say whether or how far the group had any direct influence on policy. The ideas and information we considered were all in the public domain, through government or the members' own publications, and similar ideas were being discussed in other settings. The group had no status or authority, and any ideas which emerged from it had to be tested in the ordinary policy-making process, including with ministers, but I think I can say that my colleagues and I were better informed, had a clearer understanding of the issues and were more confident in the arguments we used, than we might have been otherwise.

---

17. Roy King and Kathleen McDermott, *The State of our Prisons*, Oxford University Press, 1995, 3-4.

CHAPTER 6

Managing the System

This and the next three chapters discuss the issues with which I was especially concerned during the period from 1982 to 1990. Most of them are still as important, and as intractable, in 2014 as they were then. This chapter is concerned with the management and organization of the criminal justice services and with sentencing. *Chapter 7* deals with probation and the probation service, and *Chapter 8* with the wider responses to crime. *Chapter 9* considers the policies towards crime and criminal justice as they became consolidated after the 1987 general election, including the preparations for the Criminal Justice Act 1991. I have not discussed the other important events that were taking place at the same time but with which I was not so closely involved — the disturbances in Brixton and other places in 1981; the Scarman inquiry which followed; the report from the Royal Commission on Criminal Procedure and the Police leading to Criminal Evidence Act 1984; the Public Order Act 1986; or the continuing struggle for power between Prison Service management and the Prison Officers' Association and the means of containing the continuing pressures on prison capacity.

The Criminal Justice System

The term 'criminal justice system' had begun to appear during the 1970s; it now came into regular use. The services and institutions involved in detecting crime and administering justice are closely inter-related and what one does can affect any or all of the others; we were especially conscious of the need to achieve a closer alignment between demand and capacity, most obviously for places in prisons but also for other services, and it was natural that a government committed to efficiency, economy and effectiveness should want it to be 'managed as a system'. We were also aware of the lack of communication between services, between services and government, and between government departments themselves,, the problem of what later became called 'silos'.[1] We were concerned about the apparent waste of resources resulting from their failure to cooperate or to understand one another's difficulties or points of view, and the services themselves were showing growing interest in the 'interdependence' of the criminal justice services, including the courts and the practising legal profession.

The ideal would have been a self-regulating system with built-in checks and balances which the Treasury hoped could be achieved with the help a mathematical model resembling the one they were constructing of the national economy. That vision was unrealistic; it could not easily be reconciled with the principle of judicial independence or the independence police or prosecutors; and for prisons it would have required politically unacceptable procedures such as executive release from prisons or offenders 'queuing' for space to become available. Some critics went further and said that the principles of judicial and operational independence meant that criminal justice was not a system, and could not and constitutionally should not be treated and still less managed as if it were one. When I described what we were doing to an audience in the United States in 1984 the American scholar Malcolm Feeley commented drily, 'We set up our country so that you couldn't do that'.

As so often, progress was more likely to be made through local consultation and goodwill than by direction or micro-management on the part of central government. We made a naïve attempt to set up a coordinating committee to discuss and resolve the various 'rubbing points', most of which were in the process of bringing defendants to trial, the listing of court business, escorts to and from prisons, the cost and sometimes injustice of delays, and the enforcement of fines and other court orders. The first meeting showed that those attending had come with a list of the demands they wanted to make and had not much interest in listening to the difficulties experienced by others. The attempt was not repeated and we looked for other, more subtle, methods. More promising developments were the later initiatives for partnerships, joint working and the formation of area criminal justice committees, but the growing culture of targets, restrictive budgets, individual

---

1. On one occasion, at a lunch with local practitioners, I discovered that the police commander, the chief prosecutor, the justices' clerk, the chairman of the magistrates, the chief probation officer and the prison governor were in many instances meeting each other for the first time.

performance and assessment (and sometimes blame) was already beginning to work against them. Economies such as restricting defendants' rights to trial at the Crown Court and therefore before a jury, or abolishing jury trial for complicated cases of fraud,[2] were considered but not pursued.

We arranged a series of conferences to bring together the three 'operational' criminal justice services—police, prisons and probation—hoping to break down the suspicion and rivalries which existed between them. Those rivalries were demonstrated at the first conference where the police arrived in uniform, the Prison Service in suits and the probation service in informal clothes, all determined to assert their identity, and so reinforcing the other services' stereotypes of themselves. There were no women, and no-one who was black or Asian. From that revealing but inauspicious start, later conferences became more inclusive and constructive, reflecting the changing and sometimes converging cultures of the three services, and especially of police and probation as police became more of a social service and probation more of an agency of law enforcement.

Within Whitehall we held regular 'trilateral' meetings with colleagues in the Lord Chancellor's Department, led by Raymond Potter, and later with the Crown Prosecution Service to coordinate policy, legislation and budgets across the three departments, exchange information and establish personal relationships. Similar, less frequent, meetings were held at Permanent Secretary and at middle-management level. I would have liked to find some means by which departments and services could have some financial benefit from cooperating with one another—co-operation always seemed to be for someone else's benefit and never for one's own—but shared budgets, for example, were always out of reach[3] and said to be in conflict with fundamental principles of government accounting and financial control.

The aim was by all those means to achieve a continuous dialogue, not confined to formal processes of consultation. More structured arrangements followed—the Criminal Justice Consultative Council and area committees, set up following the Woolf report in 1991 (see *Chapter 9*); the more limited

---

2. As recommended by the Roskill Report (Fraud Trials Committee Report), London: HMSO, 1986. The Report led to the establishment of the Serious Fraud Office in 1988.

3. Although there had once been a precedent in the single budget which several departments had shared for home defence.

Trials Issues Group, set up in 1997; and the Cabinet Office Committee on Crime and the Criminal Justice System.

Sentencing and the Treatment of Offenders

It must now be hard to realise how far the Home Office approach to criminal justice was throughout the 1970s and 1980s dominated by concern for the size of the prison population and by the danger of losing control of one or more prisons, whether because of disturbances by prisoners or industrial action by prison officers. Any change of policy or practice had to be considered from the point of view of its effect on the prison population, (although drugs were an exception — see *Chapter 8*). Michael Zander argued in his bicentenary lecture for a system of regular executive release and that 'nothing less will be enough to meet the situation'. An unfortunate consequence was that any discussion of the limitations of imprisonment as a means of rehabilitating offenders or reducing crime, the scope for more promising alternatives, or the damage caused to prisoners' families and their communities, could be (and often still is) dismissed as a cynical attempt to save money. The precarious state of the prison system could potentially do immense political damage to the government, and disorder or industrial action might eventually lead to the ultimate humiliation of large scale executive release. That possibility was never far from our minds. But we were always aware of the criticism that any attempt to reduce the use of imprisonment was likely to provoke, and we thought we were more likely to make progress gradually, through a series of 'grandmother's footsteps', than by a dramatic initiative or high profile campaign.

For the first part of the 1980s, criminal justice policies followed the usual pattern of handling situations and responding to events. Changes were made in the administration of parole and life sentences (see below). For prisoners whose sentence was too short to qualify for release on parole, a proposal for administrative early release under supervision was canvassed for possible inclusion in the Bill for the Criminal Justice Act 1982, but under pressure from the judges it was soon abandoned. The 1982 Act did however begin a process of rationalising the sentencing arrangements for young offenders, including the abolition of the sentence of borstal training as the Advisory Council on the Penal System had recommended in 1974 (see *Chapter 2*), although detention centres remained as separate institutions, with a separate sentence, until 1988. It set out for the first time restrictive criteria for the use of custodial sentences which were carried forward in the Criminal Justice Act 1988 and pointed towards the more comprehensive provisions in the Criminal Justice Act 1991. The 1982 Act also removed the penalty of imprisonment for the offences of begging and soliciting for prostitution, although that was more symbolic than the start of any programme of depenalisation. Ministers were interested in schemes of day or weekend imprisonment as a means of reducing the pressure on prisons, but after much discussion they accepted that intermittent custody would not be practicable in the country.

Some commentators have thought of the 1980s as an Indian summer of liberal criminal justice policy, in contrast to the blizzard of punitive legislation which followed, but there were already signs of a change in political and probably public attitudes. Other provisions in the Criminal Justice Acts of 1987 and 1988 pointed in a different direction: increased the maximum sentences for firearms offences, cruelty to children, corruption and insider dealing; a power for the Attorney General to refer apparently over-lenient sentences to the Court of Appeal with a view to having them increased; majority verdicts in jury trials; restrictions on the suspect's or defendant's right of silence under questioning and, following the Roskill report, new arrangements for fraud trials, although without the abolition of jury trial which the report had favoured. References to the Court of Appeal and majority verdicts by juries were in response to a strong demand from the Lord Chief Justice, Lord Lane, and from the judiciary more generally, and restrictions on the right of silence in response to pressure from the police. We hesitated over all of them, and I was especially concerned that references to the Court of Appeal would be used more in response to pressure from the public, newspapers or victims than from a dispassionate review of the case; but in the climate at the time it was difficult to advance arguments of principle and we were keen to have the judiciary's support, or at least to avoid their hostility, for what we saw as the more important issues of sentencing and the use of imprisonment. I wondered if the change might lead to a role for the prosecution in advising the judge on sentencing, and whether I would welcome it if it did, but the idea was never pursued.

The experimental 'tougher regimes' in detention centres had a short life, but when Leon Brittan became Home Secretary he introduced more restrictive criteria for the grant of parole (see below), essentially as a means of strengthening his position in the Conservative party, and ministers began to increase the 'tariff' (the minimum term to be spent in custody) for life sentence prisoners above the length which the sentencing judge had recommended and to substitute a longer period based on their judgement of the political sensitivity of the offence. Leon Brittan also introduced the consideration of 'public confidence' into the process of policy-making, where it has been a major factor since that time. At first I saw it and argued for it as an argument for good practice—making sure that the system was accountable, that what was supposed to happen did happen, that people knew where they stood and felt they were being treated fairly and with respect. In the event, 'public confidence' gradually turned into an argument for convicting more offenders and for greater severity in sentencing, and led to the 'penal populism' which became characteristic of both Conservative and Labour parties during the 1990s and subsequently.[4]

A new emphasis on punishment began to emerge, for example in speeches by John Patten[5] and in the use of the expression 'punishment in the community'. It was intended at first to indicate that imprisonment was not the only sentence which counted as 'punishment' and to counter the impression that to receive any other order or sentence was to be 'let off'. There was however a growing expectation and later insistence that any wrongdoing had to be punished in a way which was somehow painful or humiliating and for which suspended sentences and probation or community service orders did not count—see below.

Parole
Parole had been introduced in 1967 as a form of early release from prison intended to help the rehabilitation of medium and long sentence prisoners

---

4. See for example Anthony Bottoms 'The Philosophy and Politics of Punishment in Sentencing' in Christopher Clarkson and Rod Morgan (eds.), *The Politics of Sentencing*, Oxford University Press, 1995. Speaking in the House of Lords in 1991, Lord Hailsham said 'Populism is the enemy of justice, the enemy of freedom, and ultimately the enemy of democracy'. Parliamentary Debates HL 528 (5th ser) col 639. 30 April, 1991.
5. See Lord Windlesham, *Responses to Crime*, Vol 2, *Penal Policy in the Making*, Oxford: Clarendon Press, 1993, pages 226-227.

who had good prospects of doing well after they left prison. Prison governors and penal reformers had welcomed it at the time. Release was at the discretion of the Secretary of State on the advice of the Parole Board. The Board was highly regarded, membership was a much sought after position, and judges who became members of the Parole Board gained a valuable insight into prison facts of life. But it involved a lot of effort, both for board members and for the secretariat, and the work was often in arrears with damaging consequences including delaying prisoners' dates of release. The process was complicated, time-consuming and difficult for prisoners to understand; it involved difficult judgements of probabilities and risk, based on what was usually uncertain evidence; prisoners often thought it was unfair; and the interface with sentencing could cause anomalies for the courts. Although the judiciary were represented on the Parole Board, it was in affect a form of executive interference with the court's decision. The courts were not supposed to take account of parole in sentencing but there was evidence (and it was hardly surprising) that they sometimes did. Governments have always tried to treat sentencing, parole, and the administration of life sentences as separate issues — sentencing for the judiciary, parole and life sentences as a matter of prison administration and therefore for the executive, but the attempt to keep them separate has always brought trouble.

The new criteria for the grant of parole brought with them a fresh set of anomalies in the relationship between parole and sentencing. In particular, a reduction in the period before a prisoner could be considered for parole enabled those serving longer sentences to be released earlier than prisoners whose sentences were too short to make them eligible for parole. Those anomalies, and increasing delays in the process, soon reached a point where it was necessary to carry out a major review. Ministers set up a committee to review the parole system under the chairmanship of Lord Carlisle,[6] primarily to resolve the anomalies which had developed as a result of earlier adjustments to the system and criticism from judges about their effect on sentencing. Its report[7] provided the basis for new arrangements and a new statutory

6. Mark Carlisle had been a founder member of the Advisory Council on the Penal System when it was re-formed in 1966, an effective junior minister at the Home Office during the 1970s, and for a time Secretary of State for Education in Margaret Thatcher's government.

7. Home Office *The Parole System in England and Wales, Report of the Review Committee* (the Carlisle Committee), Cm 532, London: HMSO, 1988.

framework which the Criminal Justice Act 1991 put in place. The committee came to the best conclusions that were possible in the circumstances, but again they were shaped by the ever-present problem of the prison population.

In later years parole was transformed from an aid to rehabilitation to an instrument for public protection, especially when it was associated with the new indeterminate sentences for public protection introduced by the Criminal Justice Act 2003 and the increasing use of life sentences and the number of life sentence prisoners. It was no longer about giving prisoners hope for the future and became an instrument for their control. Uncertainties, anomalies and delays continued, with serious injustice when prisoners were denied release because administrative obstacles prevented them from satisfying the — often artificial — criteria (such as going on a course) for deciding that they were no longer a risk to the public.

I have always doubted whether parole did very much good, either in promoting rehabilitation or in protecting the public. Even with a judge among the members of the Parole Board, I always felt uncomfortable about the legitimacy of a process affecting people's liberty which has little transparency and relies so strongly on administrative judgement and practicability. Some provision is needed for deciding on the release or continued detention of prisoners who may be too dangerous to be released at the point when their punishment would otherwise have been served, but I would prefer it to be a simpler and more limited process.

Murder and Life Imprisonment

An unwelcome distraction was a series of Parliamentary debates on the restoration of the death penalty, which the Prime Minister was known to favour. Whitelaw was at first disposed to take a neutral position, setting out the facts and the arguments but leaving the House of Commons to decide. In the event, having seen the material that was provided for him, he decided that he should advise the House against restoration. That view prevailed in Parliament, then and in subsequent debates although as Home Secretary in 1983 Leon Brittan felt that he had to speak in favour of a limited restoration out of loyalty to the Prime Minister.

Murder has always been seen, politically and to a large extent by the public, as the most heinous of all crimes and as needing to be marked by an exceptional sentence—at one time death and now the mandatory sentence of life imprisonment. And yet the definition of murder includes a wide range of actions and intentions which are not usually seen as the most wicked that can be committed (mercy killing is the usual example), and as less serious than some which would attract a less severe maximum penalty. The mandatory sentence prevents judges from taking different degrees of harm or culpability into account, and results in an elaborate process of judgement and risk assessment before release can be authorised.

The definition of murder and the mandatory life sentence raise practical concerns for the Prison Service about the way in which prisoners serving sentences are to be treated, but also issues of principle for the relationship between the judiciary and the executive. They have been present ever since the Murder (Abolition of Death Penalty) Act 1965 and the compromises that were reached to secure the passage of the Bill, but successive governments have so far refused to engage in serious discussion at a political or Parliamentary level. Similar problems arise, although to a lesser degree, for the discretionary life sentences which judges may impose for crimes less serious than murder. The subject is discussed in Chapter 7 of Volume 2 of Lord Windlesham's *Responses to Crime*,[8] and more comprehensively by Terence Morris and Louis Blom-Cooper in their book *Fine Lines and Distinctions*.[9]

During my time in the Prison Department the comparatively small number of life sentence prisoners (under 3,000) were managed by the 'Lifer Section' at headquarters, under the oversight of an administrative Life Sentence Board chaired by the Permanent Secretary. Great attention was paid to safety and security, but the underlying purpose was to enable prisoners to progress through greater levels of responsibility and lower degrees of security to an open prison and eventually to release on licence. It was acknowledged that some prisoners might never be released but it was taken for granted that the possibility should not be formally excluded.

Following the defeat of the attempt to restore the death penalty in 1983, Leon Brittan announced to the Conservative Party Conference that regardless of the judges' recommendations those guilty of certain categories of murder

---

8.   n4, pages 308-346.
9.   Terence Morris and Louis Blom-Cooper, *Fine Lines and Distinctions: Murder, Manslaughter and the Unlawful Taking of Human Life*, Sherfield-on-Loddon: Waterside Press, 2011.

should automatically serve a minimum of 20 years before being considered for release. He also instituted a system of setting the minimum period by an administrative process in which the decision was to be taken by a minister. The decision would be taken on grounds of 'public confidence' rather than the degree of punishment which the person deserved or the risk they might be to the public, and the terms set were often considerably longer than those which the judge had recommended.

Tension between the judges and the Home Office inevitably followed, with a series of judgements in the Divisional Court, a report from a House of Lords Select Committee chaired by Lord Nathan,[10] and then a judgement by the European Court of Human Rights,[11] all of which asserted that release should be a judicial decision taken by a judge and not an executive decision taken by a minister. An accommodation was reached in Section 34 of the Criminal Justice Act 1991 under which the Secretary of State would release a prisoner serving a discretionary life sentence at the point recommended by the judge, but ministers insisted on keeping political control of those serving mandatory sentences. An unfounded and misguided belief grew up that the compulsory life sentence introduced when the death penalty was abolished constituted some kind of 'pact' between Parliament and the public which must be preserved in perpetuity.[12] In the Criminal Justice Act 2003 the Labour government added the possibility of a 'whole life' sentence from which there would be no possibility of release; and the Coalition government's Legal Aid, Sentencing and Punishment of Offenders Act 2012 extended mandatory sentences of life imprisonment from murder to those convicted a second time for serious sexual and violent offences.

Soon after leaving the Home Office I was asked to become a member of the Committee on the Penalty for Homicide, set up by the Prison Reform Trust and chaired by Lord Lane who had by then retired as Lord Chief Justice. I had no difficulty in supporting the committee's conclusion[13] that

---

10. House of Lords, Session 1988/89 *Report of the Select Committee on Murder and Life Imprison-ment* (HL Paper 78), London: HMSO, 1989

11. *Thynne, Wilson and Gunnell v The United Kingdom* (1991) 13 ECHR 135.

12. Terence Morris and Louis Blom-Cooper (n7, pages 188-189) say that the 'pact' originated in 1995 but others recall it as having appeared at the time of Leon Brittan's changes to the administration of life sentences in 1983.

13. Prison Reform Trust, *Committee on the Penalty for Murder,* London: Prison Reform Trust, 1993.

sentencing is a function of the courts and that life imprisonment should be the maximum but not the mandatory penalty for murder, but no government since the abolition of the death penalty has felt able to resist the temptation to introduce further legislation or administrative changes in the operation of the life sentence.

Crown Prosecution Service

Two major Acts of Parliament were the Police and Criminal Evidence Act 1984 (PACE) and the Prosecution of Offences Act 1985. Both arose from the report of the Royal Commission on Criminal Procedure. The transformation of police procedure which came to be enacted in PACE was a matter for the Police Department and I was not much involved, but the recommendation for the creation of a prosecution service independent of the police fell to the Criminal Department.

There was general support for making the prosecution process independent, as a matter of both practice and principle, but no consensus on the structure for the new arrangements. The Royal Commission had recommended a system which would be locally based alongside police services, but others favoured a national service which would be more able to ensure consistency and be more effectively insulated from local political interference. Bill Bohan and Joan McNaughton took the lead within the Home Office, and after a good deal of discussion we decided to recommend to the Home Secretary, now Leon Brittan, a unified service headed by the Director of Public Prosecutions and accountable to the Attorney General. It was a departure from my usual preference for local arrangements wherever possible, but we thought a national service would not only be more likely to achieve consistency and more genuinely independent, but more able to contribute to the developing arrangements for cooperation and coordination across the system and for managing it 'as a whole'.

I was interested in particular in the lessons that might be learned from procurators fiscal in Scotland, the prosecution service in The Netherlands (for example their use of prosecution fines), and district attorneys in the

United States.[14] Ministers agreed, and the Prosecution of Offences Act 1985, was framed accordingly.

The change to a national service was a difficult process. The consultants who designed the transition had to disentangle the cost of the previous arrangements from that of police services as a whole, and make an estimate of what the cost of the new service would be. The cost was underestimated, and the service was at first was seriously underfunded. Its early years were also marked by clashes of personality among those who had been prominent local figures in the past. I wondered for a time whether we had made the right decision, but in retrospect I am sure that we did.

I wondered whether the formation of the Crown Prosecution Service, together with the provision for it, through the Attorney General, to refer apparently over-lenient sentences to the Court of Appeal and the development of sentencing guidelines (at first from the Court of Appeal, later from the Sentencing Council and its predecessors) would in time lead to the prosecution having a role in sentencing. That would have enabled the judge to hear arguments about the appropriate sentence from both sides, and it might have resulted in sentences for which the reasons for them were more transparent and more readily perceived to be fair, but the argument never made any progress.

New Technology

The enthusiasm for new technology which had been a feature of the 1960s was not at first repeated with the technology that was becoming available in the 1980s. I shared the general approval for its use for the security of property and vehicles, and for personal safety (although drawing the line at some of the potentially dangerous devices that were acceptable in the United States). For those purposes it came to form a major part of the crime prevention programme. I saw the value of CCTV although I was sceptical about the scale on which it came to be installed. I welcomed electronic management and communication systems, although the problems which seem to beset all

---

14. In Oakland, California, I was able to observe a regular morning meeting between the district attorney and the police commander at which they reviewed the defendants who had been arrested on the previous day and reached a pragmatic agreement on those who should be released with a suitable warning and those who should be taken to court.

government computer systems were already becoming apparent. The high point of enthusiasm for the police had however already passed with the realisation that technology is not a substitute for human contact and individual judgement. Its successful use required a clear understanding of the context, of its relationships and dynamics, and of the purposes for which it was to be employed, and that understanding was too often absent. Technology might make a solution possible but it would not in itself provide a solution to a problem, and it could never be substitute for human judgement or relationships.

There were enthusiasts for the electronic monitoring of offenders, and some who hoped that it might help to provide a credible 'alternative to prison', but the prevailing view was that while electronic monitoring could be useful to support a court order and a probation officer's authority, and may encourage self-discipline and a stable lifestyle, it should not be used as a punishment in itself.

The development about which I felt most troubled was not one of government policy but the use of technology by property developers and property managers to create gated residential estates and private spaces in shopping centres and other places, often with elaborate systems for surveillance and controlling access, privately owned and policed and with the implication of a divided, anxious and suspicious society. Associated with it was the formation of a 'mercenary' force of private security personnel, employed by large private and often international companies, working on the boundary of the state but outside its systems of accountability and democratic control. Like the practice of contracting-out prisons and outsourcing other criminal justice services, it is an aspect of the 'market state' to which I return in *Chapter 12*.

CHAPTER 7

Probation and the Probation Service

The Probation Service mattered to the government because it held the key to limiting the size of the prison population. It still had strong support among many magistrates and in the House of Lords, but its social work ethos, its 'liberal' tradition and its reputation for weak management made support for probation difficult for ministers. In 1982 the situation was not helped by a bitter dispute with the National Association of Probation Officers (NAPO) over the pay of trainee probation officers, and NAPO made no secret of its dislike of the Thatcher government and all it stood for. The future of the service was precarious,[1] as it has been ever since. The service and the Home Office had to respond, both politically and also for the service's own professional integrity and credibility.

Tension and Conflict

The developments in after-care, parole and community service had transformed the nature and volume of the work the service had to do, and in many ways the character of the service itself. It was poised awkwardly between contrasting and often conflicting ideas of its identity and purpose. Ministers wanted it to develop 'tougher' programmes and methods of supervision to satisfy the public's demands for punishment, and to provide sentencing options for 'punishment in the community' which the courts would find more attractive than imprisonment. They also wanted the service to be more efficient and economical and more effectively managed, and to be more closely integrated with the rest of the criminal justice system. Probation committees, composed mainly of magistrates but including a Crown Court judge and co-opted members, were the service's employers but more a forum for discussion than an effective mechanism of governance or accountability.

---

1.   See for example Lord Windlesham, *Responses to Crime*, Vol 2, *Penal Policy in the Making*, Oxford: Clarendon Press, 1993, pages 225-229.

The probation inspectorate[2] had been more occupied with the selection and training of the staff and the general wellbeing of the service than with standards of performance and quantifiable results. Some probation officers still saw their primary job as being to 'advise, assist and befriend' offenders and certainly not to punish them, and thought of themselves as individual practitioners, loosely coordinated by their chief and senior officers but not to be 'managed' in the sense of having set tasks to be carried out according to set standards or of being held accountable for their performance.

Most chief officers recognised the need for stronger management, many were attracted by the prospect of a more central and perhaps more powerful role for the service, and all probation staff were happy to do what they could to reduce the use of imprisonment. They were however concerned that they should not have to sacrifice their core values of humanity and compassion for offenders and respect for their identity and dignity, and they saw a risk that the service might become just another agency of law enforcement, not significantly different in character from the police or prison services, and that its wider, less well-defined but perhaps no less important contribution to the resettlement of offenders, and to social wellbeing more generally, would be neglected. They wanted the service to retain its earlier character as a social work agency, working with and behalf of offenders and doing its best for them, and also engaging with their families and with local communities more generally. They were afraid that it might cease to be a graduate service with a distinctive professional identity of its own, and that it might no longer have, or be thought to need, skills or qualifications above a basic level of competence.

The service could not however afford to be seen as precious or complacent, as being 'on the side' of the offender, or as 'good guys' in contrast to the 'bad guys' in the police and prison services. Its accountability had to be primarily to the courts and the public, and not to the offender. It had to reconcile itself to its role in punishment. The use of the word 'client' was not politically acceptable and 'offender' was to be used instead.[3] The

---

2.   The Ministry of Justice has published a history of the Inspectorate, available at http://www.justice.gov.uk/downloads/about/hmiprob/history-hmi-probation.pdf

3.   Although 'offender' was itself open to objection if it was used in effect to define a person's identity.

expression 'punishment in the community', favoured by ministers, raised concerns not only for probation officers but also among scholars such as David Garland and Barbara Hudson about the political attitudes and the kind of society it seemed to reflect, but the expression, and words such as 'tough' and 'demanding' that were associated with it, served a necessary purpose in emphasising that imprisonment was not the only sentence which counted as punishment. I rationalised its use, perhaps rather disingenuously, by suggesting that it might help to reinforce communities' own responsibilities for its social misfits and failures.

I was concerned that the service should still retain its separate identity within the criminal justice system, and so far as possible its social work tradition. I spoke of it as a 'criminal justice agency with a social work base', preserving its values of humanity, compassion and respect—although those were not unique to the probation service, as some probation officers seemed to believe—and working with families, victims and communities where possible. In that role it had sponsored the first victim support schemes, it was now promoting some of the first ventures in restorative justice, and it was beginning to play a part in crime prevention (see *Chapter 8*). That was potentially important, pioneering work, but it did not have much resonance with ministers' priorities, then or subsequently.

The Policy Evolves

There was a short period in which the Home Office relaxed some of its central control as part of the Conservative government's commitment to reducing bureaucracy and 'red tape', for example over the approval of some appointments. We soon adopted a more assertive approach, both to comply with the government's Financial Management Initiative and to make the service more effective in the work we wanted it to do. In consultation with the service's then representative organizations (Association of Chief Officers of Probation (ACOP), NAPO and the Central Council of Probation Committees) we drew up a set of national standards and practice guidelines, and in due course a system of 'cash limits' was applied to probation as it was to other public services. Probation committees were asked to reform their procedures and to hold their area services more rigorously to account for their expenditure and performance. The Home Office became fully responsible for funding the service, ending the 20 per cent contribution from local authorities and with it—I later thought regrettably—the stake which they had held in their local service. Following a review in 1987 the inspectorate was given a new role of inspecting the service's performance against the national standards which were then in place. In the Criminal Justice Act 1991 it was placed on a statutory basis alongside the inspectorate of prisons and also with the pre-fix 'Her Majesty's'. Further changes followed critical reports[4] from the National Audit Office and the Audit Commission in 1989, dealing with the structure of the service and the management of its processes respectively. To show that it was a punishment, the probation order became a sentence of the court instead of an alternative to a sentence, and it no longer required the person's consent (Section 8 Criminal Justice 1991).

I accepted that those changes were necessary if the probation service was to have the confidence of ministers and the credibility to do the work which was now expected and to make the contribution to social cohesion and social justice of which it was capable. Subject to a few reservations, I was comfortable in pressing them forward. I did however see a need for a more strategic, and if possible more optimistic, sense of direction and purpose, which would be shared by the service and the Home Office and recognised and respected by the courts and other criminal justice services. My first thought was that it might be expressed in a national statement which I hoped could be agreed and owned jointly by the service's representative organizations and the Home Office. That proved unrealistic, perhaps not surprisingly, and after consultation the Home Office issued its own more limited and more managerial Statement of National Objectives and Priorities (SNOP) instead.

The statement emphasised the need for efficient and effective use of resources and the place of the service within the wider criminal justice system, and its reports to the courts and the supervision of those offenders for whom it was compulsory[5] as its most important functions. Local probation areas were later asked to draw up their own statements of local objectives and priorities, to be approved by their probation committees and submitted to

4.   National Audit Office, *Home Office Control and Management of Probation Services in England and Wales,* London: HMSO, 1989; Audit Commission, *The Probation Service: Promoting Value for Money,* London: HMSO, 1989.
5.   Those subject to court orders such as probation and community service, or to compulsory supervision after serving sentences of 12 months or more.

the Home Office. One casualty was the voluntary after-care of short sentence prisoners not subject to compulsory supervision which was given low priority in the national and local statements. Another was work with families, victims (for example restorative justice) and communities. The pressure continued with the cuts in expenditure that were imposed during the following years, and the concentration on office-based activities that could more easily be measured — appointments made and kept, sessions provided and attended for drug or alcohol treatment, programmes completed

Leadership and Innovation

The service's leaders during that period included Michael Day,[6] Cedric Fullwood, John Harding, Anne Mace, Jenny Roberts[7] and Roger Statham, and also Colin Thomas and Graham Smith who later became chief inspectors of probation and Breidge Gadd in Northern Ireland. The 1980s and 1990s were a period of sometimes painful questioning and adjustment. The points of tension related both to reforms of management and to the government's increasing emphasis on punishment. To those between care and control, rehabilitation and punishment, and the interests of the offender and those of the public were now added those between the offender and the victim. They all became more salient, and more difficult to resolve, as the service's role became more prominent and exposed.

Despite and in some ways because of the political and managerial tensions, the period was also one of practical innovation and creative thought, inspired both by the service's own leaders and the growing number of probation scholars in universities, many of whom had themselves served as probation officers. Practical innovations included day centres, bail information schemes and groupwork; there was increasing interest in evidence-based practice, often based on services' own research and management information; and the service began to form partnerships with voluntary organizations in providing support for offenders. Chris Stone from the Vera Institute of Justice in New York (see *Chapter 5*) was a valuable interpreter and catalyst.

6.　Later Chair of the Commission for Racial Equality.

7.　Jenny Roberts later founded, and Colin Thomas edited, the probation journal *Vista*, now *Eurovista*, as a vehicle for publishing the kinds of articles that began to appear at that time. I was a member of the editorial board.

More theoretical debates took place at conferences and in articles in journals by writers such as Bill McWilliams, Mike Nellis, John Pendleton, Peter Raynor, Philip Whitehead and Maurice Vanstone. They brought new ideas to the management of the service and re-examined the underlying fundamental questions about the nature and purpose of criminal justice and of punishment and the service's role in relation to them. The service's perspective was well-expressed in the three sets of papers edited by Roger Shaw and Kevin Haines, Roger Statham and Philip Whitehead and David Ward and Malcolm Lacey.[8] They were important and stimulating debates, but probation officers still had to be careful not to give an impression, especially to ministers, that they were more interested in intellectual argument than in 'fighting crime'.

The service was at a disadvantage in not having a single, recognised national leader. In 1982 chief officers formed the Association of Chief Officers of Probation to give stronger professional leadership to the service and to represent its managers more effectively at national level. It replaced their previous, less formal, Conference of Chief Probation Officers and the Home Office provided the funds for a small staff. The association quickly established itself and became influential, both within the service and nationally, but the chair was never a full-time appointment—he or she was 'first among equals' and held office for only one year. The structure did not provide for any equivalent of the director general of the Prison Service and there was—and still is—no acknowledged person of authority who is a public figure able to represent the service as a whole. ACOP never had the same influence as the Association of Chief Police Officers, but was however able to engage more effectively than before with ministers, other government departments, the Magistrates' Association and the Justices' Clerks Society.[9]

In the 1990s Graham Smith became in effect the national leader of the service in his role as HM Chief Inspector of Probation, but probation was

8.   See for example Roger Shaw and Kevin Haines (eds.), *The Criminal Justice System: A Central Role for the Probation Service,* Cambridge Institute of Criminology, 1989; Roger Statham and Philip Whitehead (eds.), *Managing the Probation Service: Issues for the 1990s,* London: Longman, 1992; and David Ward and Malcolm Lacey (eds.), *Probation: Working for Justice,* London: Whiting and Birch, 1995.

9.   Michael Day has recently written (in personal correspondence) 'Perhaps it was a time when there was a real sense of shared purpose between all parties and ACOP certainly had ease of access to ministers as well as, when necessary, other departments of state. Civil servants... were supportive of the service's aspirations.'

not thought to need the degree of protection for decency and human rights that was required for custodial institutions. The Probation inspectorate never achieved the same degree of independence or authority as the inspectorate of prisons. Graham Smith and his team had to show that probation 'works' in terms that were acceptable to ministers,[10] and he succeeded in keeping the service in being at a time when its existence had come to be in danger, but unlike HM Chief Inspector of Prisons he had to act more as an agent of the government than as an independent authority.

Hopes and Prospects

I set out my ideas for the future of the service at a Clarke Hall conference in Cambridge in July, 1989.[11] Although the talk had the title 'The Future of the Probation Service: A View from Government' it was essentially my own vision. I discussed the service's identity as an agency of the criminal justice system with a social work base and what that implied; its role in punishment; the importance of its credibility and effectiveness in responding to crime and especially in reducing reoffending; issues of performance measurement, management and leadership; and the distinction between functions which the service had to carry out itself and those which might be performed by others. On punishment I said that it was imposed by the court and not by the Probation Service; it was the loss of liberty or opportunity required by the sentence not an activity or form of treatment that was somehow added on to it and intended to be degrading or humiliating for its own sake. I went on to say that it must not mean rejection. The person should retain their own identity and their place in society and the responsibilities that went with it should be restored as soon as possible.

There was not yet a strong political emphasis on reducing reoffending and ministers, officials and the service were still sceptical about how realistic that would be, but I said

---

10. Drawing for example on Andrew Underdown's work on cognitive behaviour, later published as *Strategies for Effective Offender Supervision*, London: Home Office, 1998. He was and assistant chief probation officer in Manchester, subsequently seconded to the Probation Inspectorate.

11. The papers for the conference were edited by Roger Shaw and Kevin Haines and published in *The Criminal Justice System: A Central Role for the Probation Service*, Cambridge Institute of Criminology, 1989.

'The service — and behind the service the Home Office and the rest of the system — must set ourselves the explicit task of reducing reoffending. I know that success cannot be guaranteed and I acknowledge the service's concern that it should not be "set up to fail". But if you and the Home Office are to be taken seriously, we must commit ourselves to the attempt.'

I would say the same things today. What I said about reoffending would now be commonplace, but what I said about punishment would not be politically acceptable to any of the main political parties.

The next few years were a period of optimism for the Probation Service. The political prominence of non-custodial penalties, reinforced by the Criminal Justice Act 1991, suggested that the service would have the opportunity, and be encouraged, to develop its skills and techniques in a broadly 'liberal' spirit, and that it could have an influential and secure position for some time to come.

Later Developments: Structure and Contracting-out

Many people thought a closer connection between the Prison and Probation Services would be logical and the generic term 'corrections' was widely used in the United States, but there was no pressure for the Probation Service to be more closely integrated with the Prison Service until the Labour government took office in 1997. The Probation Service would have objected strongly, and the Prison Service had for some years had to concentrate on its own internal management, on controlling its overcrowded population, and on improving its working practices and in particular its relations with the Prison Officers' Association. It had little interest in work outside its own institutions. A higher priority was to achieve better communications and a more sympathetic understanding between the two services as part of my wider attempts to improve the working of the system as a whole. I believed that, professionally and constitutionally, probation should be aligned more with the courts and local authority services than with a centralised, monolithic national organization which was part of central government.

The green paper *Punishment, Custody and the Community*.[12] (see *Chapter 9*) raised the possibility that some functions would be contracted out to other

---

12.   Home Office *Punishment, Custody and the Community* (Cm 424). London: HMSO, 1988.

organizations. I said in my Clarke Hall lecture that there are some functions which should unquestionably remain with the Probation Service, such as reports to court, the supervision and enforcement of orders (what later became known as 'offender management') and proceedings for breach of an order. Others were clearly not for the service but for the relevant agency or institution — education classes and industrial workshops were examples. Between them were accommodation schemes, employment services, drug and alcohol groups, day centres and some types of community service where it was not obvious that the probation service should be the direct or only provider where others might have better skills or more experience. I said, provocatively at the time, that the service should resist the temptation to think that if there is a task to be done, it has to do it itself; there was a danger of dissipating its skills and overloading its management, and a more relevant skill for the service might be in assembling packages, coordinating services provided by others and seeing that collectively they achieved the right results. I was thinking primarily of the voluntary sector and of local, ad hoc arrangements between probation services and voluntary organizations in their area: I did not envisage commercial businesses being run for profit or large national contracts.[13]

The suggestion in the green paper was not seriously pursued for another 20 years, and the plans for 'transforming rehabilitation' which the Coalition government announced in 2013[14] go much further than anything I contemplated in 1989. I return to the subject of contracting-out and commissioning in *Chapter 11*.

In later years, as a non-executive director of a NHS community health trust, I several times accompanied health visitors on their visits to patients' homes. I was impressed by the extent to which they could, and often did, provide a social service to their communities which went well beyond a strict definition of their role. I saw that service as having great value for troubled

---

13. In 1992 Mary Fielder explored the implications and the lessons to be learned from experience in America, drawing attention to issues such as accountability, professional training, culture and identity, continuity and stability of provision, and the special difficulties which would face the voluntary sector. 'Purchasing and Providing Services for Offenders: Lessons from America' in *Managing the Probation Service: Issues for the 1990s* — n6, 163-172. Her concerns are even more relevant today.

14. Home Office, *Transforming Rehabilitation: A Strategy for Reform,* London: Stationery Office, 2013.

families and households where several members were having problems of different kinds,[15] although it was becoming hard to reconcile that kind of service with the culture of targets and performance indicators which had then become prevalent. I saw a comparison with the potential work of the Probation Service, and wished it could have been possible for the service to develop in that direction instead of becoming an increasingly office-bound agency of punishment and law enforcement.

15. The human misery I observed in a travelling family in rural Oxfordshire was greater than any I had seen in the troubled areas of big cities.

CHAPTER 8

Wider Responses to Crime

This chapter deals with responses to crime, and with issues of social order and social justice which affect the level of crime but are not, or should not be, primarily matters for the criminal process or for the criminal justice services. They were, and still are, politically sensitive but they were not for the most part those to which ministers wanted to give political prominence or with which they felt politically confident at that time.

Preventing and Reducing Crime

Crime prevention, like race relations and support for victims of crime, was not at first of much interest to ministers or to many of those in the criminal justice services. It was worthy but not exciting, rather like (as William Whitelaw once said) 'meals on wheels'. The research described in *Chapter 5* had however persuaded us that success in reducing crime depends more on action taken outside the criminal justice process than on law enforcement, sentencing or the treatment of offenders; and that more could be achieved by physical and situational measures to reduce the opportunities for crime and to make it harder to commit.

In the autumn of 1982 Brian Cubbon convened a conference at the Police College at Bramshill with representatives of the police, local authorities including their planning and housing departments, voluntary organizations and others to explore the scope for local initiatives of that kind, and at the same time established a Crime Prevention Unit to provide stimulation and support. The unit was located administratively within the Police Department in order to demonstrate that policing is about more than enforcing the law and locking up criminals, but it reported to me on policy as part of my responsibility for coordinating responses to crime.

New ideas were progressively developed and put into practice during the years which followed. Neighbourhood Watch was introduced and generally welcomed, and fears that it would lead to neighbours spying or informing on each other were not realised. Nacro was especially helpful in promoting ideas, carrying them into practical effect and demonstrating what could be done. Ministers became more interested and enthusiastic. A Standing Conference on Crime Prevention was established as a national forum, with wide membership from central and local government, the insurance and security industries and the police, and a Ministerial Group on Crime Prevention with membership from the relevant government departments. The new charity Crime Concern was established in accordance with a commitment in the Conservative party's manifesto for the 1987 election. A common theme was to work in partnership with private companies and local people to set up innovative ways of addressing crime and the fear of crime from improving people's knowledge of crime prevention. Examples included the installation of better lighting and locks; the security of vehicles, the use of CCTV; and the design and management of housing estates, football grounds and public houses. Those ideas and initiatives were brought together in 1989 by the formation of 'Secured by Design', which still continues as a group of police projects focusing on the design and security of houses, commercial premises and car parks and the quality of security products.

Defensive, physical measures had the advantage that they were tangible and visible and involved technology and hardware which the private sector was very happy to supply. I was concerned that they should if possible be complemented by social and environmental measures in which agencies and local citizens could work together. There was evidence that progress could also be made through initiatives in areas such as housing or education, perhaps using models drawn from public and environmental health. We were less successful in those areas: the evidence was less clear cut, the relevant interests both in Whitehall departments and locally nearer the ground were more firmly entrenched, and the government was firmly opposed to anything which could be labelled as 'social engineering' or as resembling the community development projects which had been promoted by the previous Labour administration.[1] A promising partnership between Nacro and the government for ex-offenders to work on crime prevention projects

---

1.   I was told that social objectives such as enabling extended families to stay in touch and support one another was no part of the government's housing policy; teachers were not social workers or police officers.

was abandoned when a newspaper gave it a headline 'jobs for yobs'.

In the summer of 1987 a group of officials spent two days at the Ship Hotel in Brighton to prepare some options which we could offer to ministers after the election. We came back with two proposals: 'Safer Cities' and 'Action for Youth'. Neither involved major programmes of public expenditure or new organizational structures. Their essence was better cooperation and understanding between statutory and voluntary services working on the ground and between government departments.

Safer Cities was a scheme for promoting initiatives by local authorities or sometimes voluntary organizations to develop a more strategic approach to crime in their areas, and the means by which authorities and agencies and local citizens could work in partnership to reduce it. The approach would cover subjects such as town planning, architectural design and public transport as well as those associated with policing and law enforcement. The scheme fitted well with the more comprehensive plans for urban regeneration which were being promoted by Michael Heseltine as 'Action for Cities', and in due course it became adopted as government policy. It was at first hampered by the Conservative government's deep-seated suspicion of local government, but it pointed towards the approach which the Labour government adopted in the Crime and Disorder Act 1998 and became the foundation for the Community Safety Partnerships (CSPs) and then the Crime and Disorder Reduction Partnerships (CDRPs) which successive governments promoted in later years.

'Action for Youth' was more difficult. We had in mind the increasing evidence, from the work of David Farrington and others, that crime runs in families, and that offending among young people is closely associated with a range of factors in their families' or households' domestic, social and economic circumstances. Similar evidence was available anecdotally from probation officers in the days when they were encouraged to visit offenders' homes and were able to gain an understanding of their family situation. The scheme we suggested would have involved centrally-guided but locally-delivered programmes of activities and interventions, targeted towards areas or groups of people where there was the greatest need but not distinguishing between those who were known offenders and those who were not. It demanded a shared objectives, performance indicators and budgets coordinated between government departments of a kind we were beginning to develop within the criminal justice sector but which had not been attempted elsewhere. It did however require an unaccustomed degree of partnership and mutual understanding between practitioners, managers and voluntary organizations which would have cut across professional and cultural as well as organizational boundaries, and the scheme did not fit the kind of 'new public management' which was being adopted across government as a whole. Above all, its support and sympathy for those suffering disadvantage did not suit the political circumstances as they were at the time.

Race and Ethnicity

Race relations were also a politically less attractive subject than law enforcement and sentencing. Ministers and many of those in the criminal justice services preferred not to think about them unless they had to. Good race relations were however a necessary part of a coherent, strategic approach to crime and to people who commit or suffer from it, and I saw it as my job to raise awareness and persuade people to take the issues seriously, as well as to help to develop the policies and practices that were necessary to tackle the substantive issues.

Evidence of racial discrimination, including powerful reports by Nacro and the experience I had already found in the Prison Service, was too strong to ignore. The urgency of the issue was demonstrated by the disturbances in Brixton, Birmingham, Liverpool and other places in 1981 and at Bridgewater Farm in London in 1985, and by the Scarman report.[2] Statistics assembled by Nacro's Race Issues Advisory Committee showed that black defendants and offenders seemed to be treated more severely than white people at every stage in the criminal justice process. The figures had a powerful impact, but many people were ready to disbelieve or ignore the evidence, or to see discrimination by others while denying it in themselves, and it prompted a reaction which claimed that black people were by their nature more criminally inclined than white people. Well-intentioned middle-class people, including those who thought of themselves as 'liberals', might agree that race relations were a problem but find it hard to accept that it had anything to

---

2.   Lord Scarman, *The Brixton Disorders 10–12 April 1981. Report of the Inquiry*, Cmnd 8427, London: HMSO.

do with them, still less that they might themselves be prejudiced. They did not see any need to question their own assumptions, stereotypes or language, and they often could not see that there was anything wrong in calling people 'coloured', or any harm in racist jokes.

Even if they accepted the need for action in principle, many of those working in criminal justice were reluctant to acknowledge the sometimes overt but more often hidden discrimination that was taking place in the police, prison and probation services and sometimes in the courts. They would try to evade the issue through protracted arguments on the detail, or by making disingenuous claims that while there might be problems in other areas or services they did not apply to themselves, for example because 'there are no black people in this area'. They were not yet ready to accept that good practice in the criminal justice sector, including of course the Home Office itself, must include understanding and respect for different cultural practices and sensibilities; sensitivity and suitable provision in matters such as language, diet, dress and religious observance; the appointment where appropriate of designated race relations officers and advisors; the recruitment, training and promotion of staff and the roles to be played by staff from minority groups; the composition of boards and committees; and ethnic monitoring. We tried to establish that view throughout the sector, building and drawing on support where we could find it including voluntary organizations and individual champions; and to sustain it through institutional arrangements where they were practicable and likely to be effective.

Progress was easier in some areas than others. There was opposition to ethnic monitoring, for example in the police, for fear of what it might reveal, and in Victim Support where many local schemes felt that people ought not as a matter of principle be identified by their race or ethnicity. Even if the case for monitoring was accepted, it was hard to find agreement on the classifications to be used. The courts were especially reluctant to accept that there could be any possibility of discrimination in the judicial process, for example as a result of insensitivity to the cultural differences in the way in which people would present themselves in court, or that any new provision could be made without interfering with the proper course of justice. The support of champions such as Rosemary Thomson at the Magistrates' Association and Lord Justice Brooke among the judges proved invaluable and helped to facilitate Roger Hood's important and influential study *Race and Sentencing*[3] and make known its results, although some Judges were for a long time reluctant to accept its finding that there was some evidence of discrimination in the Crown Court.

I hoped it would become possible to introduce a statutory provision on the lines of the Race Relations Act 1976, prohibiting discrimination in the administration of justice as it was already prohibited in the fields of employment, the provision of goods and services, education and public functions. That proved impossible at the time because neither the judiciary nor the services were willing to accept that discrimination actually existed, but we did (with difficulty) obtain agreement to the provision which became Section 95 of the Criminal Justice Act 1991. The section required the Secretary of State to 'publish such information as he considers expedient for the purpose of facilitating the performance of those engaged in the administration of justice to avoid discriminating against any persons on the ground of race or sex or any other improper ground.' The issue was at least, for the first time, recognised in legislation[4].

It was always hard to raise the subject of race without the risk of giving offence to someone or being accused of 'political correctness' (although that expression had not yet come into common use), but I thought the danger of unfair and often thoughtless discrimination should always be in people's minds. I raised it in many of my talks and speeches, and we always raised it at the criminal justice conferences described in *Chapter 9*. Too many people who should have known better, including some in high places, were still ready to make sexist or racist jokes at meetings and conferences, but most of those working in criminal justice came to acknowledge the things that needed to be done, even if they disagreed about the methods or the detail. Our aim was to reduce and eventually we hoped eliminate conscious and unconscious discrimination and prejudice, and at the same time to help members of minority groups to take a full part as citizens and members of British society while retaining their ethnic and cultural identities within it.

---

3.   Roger Hood, *Race and Sentencing*, Oxford: Clarendon Press, 1992.
4.   The Race Relations (Amendment) Act 2000 later included a statutory duty on all public bodies to promote race equality, and to demonstrate that procedures to prevent race discrimination are effective.

Whether or not as a consequence of what we did at that time, some of the worst manifestations of racism have been removed or suppressed, and I hope that members of minority groups can for the most part feel more confident about the criminal justice process than they could then. Events such as the murder of Stephen Lawrence, the failures in its investigation and Lord Macpherson's inquiry were still in the future. More needed and still needs to be done. Longstanding problems remain over police powers of 'stop and search'; there are still special difficulties in particular parts of the country and in relations between the police and some groups of individuals, for example young black men in London. Wider and sometimes more subtle and insidious issues of prejudice and discrimination continue to emerge, often arising from perceptions of difference or from immigration as well as ethnicity.

Our approach came to be characterised as 'multiculturalism' and is said to have 'failed' because some people preferred, or may for whatever reason have felt compelled, to live within their own communities without becoming part of a wider community of British citizens. No-one proposed a realistic alternative, and I would not accept that our approach was mistaken or misguided because it did not achieve all that we hoped.

I was later asked to become a member of the Commission on the Future of Multi-Ethnic Britain, set up by the Runnymede Foundation and chaired by Professor Bhikhu (now Lord) Parekh. The Commission's vision of a 'community of communities', connected by a common sense of citizenship and human rights, balancing cohesion, equality and difference and acknowledging multiple identities, corresponded with my own. I was disappointed that criticism in the *Daily Telegraph* caused the Labour government to distance itself from the report[5] when it was published in 2000, although most of its recommendations were quietly accepted during the period which followed.

Victims of Crime

Governments and services had shown a similar insouciance towards victims of crime. The neglect of victims had become recognised during the 1970s, in Great Britain though the work of probation officers and Nacro, and then by the voluntary victims' support schemes set up to respond to that concern.

---

5. Runnymede Trust, *The Future of Multi-Ethnic Britain: The Parekh Report*, London: Profile Books, 2000.

In Norway Nils Christie had written his powerful paper[6] about the 'theft of an issue' — the way in which the state's processes of justice deprive victims of 'ownership' of the means by which they can obtain justice, so that they feel powerless to take any action of their own. I had not thought much about the subject until 1982; by that time victims' support schemes had become established in most parts of the country and were coordinated by their national association, later Victim Support, but neither the movement nor the issues had so far become widely known, and support from government was now needed. Ministers and others still thought that the Criminal Injuries Compensation Scheme, introduced in 1964, did everything that victims could reasonably expect from government, and Leon Brittan, now Home Secretary and a former Chief Secretary to the Treasury, was concerned that government funding for Victim Support might become a substantial new financial commitment, perhaps leading to the formation of a new, paid social service — the last thing that the Conservative government wanted.

Many of the issues were in principle quite straightforward. Victims deserve and should receive all possible consideration and support in their contacts with the police, the courts and other criminal justice services, so far as is consistent with the requirements of justice for themselves, for defendants and offenders, and for others who may be affected. All concerned should respect victims' interests and feelings and take them into account. Victims should be able to obtain financial compensation from offenders or the state, within the limits of affordability, practicability and natural justice. More specific and less tractable issues included the treatment and sometimes humiliation of victims when giving evidence in court, and the information given to them about the progress of police investigations, prosecutions and hearings in court, or about the arrangements for a prisoner's release. There were special problems relating to victims of rape and domestic violence, and there was still a long way to go before they were properly recognised, and still further before they could be resolved.

More complex considerations arose about how far the fact of being a victim of crime gave a person's views (for example on sentencing) any special authority compared with those of anyone else; a claim for compensation or consideration different from those of others who may have suffered similar

6.   Nils Christie, 'Conflicts as Property', *British Journal of Criminology*, 17: 1-15, 1977.

injuries or misfortunes from other causes; or a special status in a criminal trial different from that of an ordinary witness. An argument that victims should be separately represented at the trial was pressed by victims' organizations in other countries and at the United Nations, but the issues were easier to resolve in a civil law than in an adversarial jurisdiction and it was not seriously pursued in the United Kingdom. In Canada and France there was for a time a campaign to establish 'victimology' as a separate academic discipline, with its own university departments and professorships. The debate had value in raising awareness and the profile of victims' issues, but there was a less helpful line of argument which presented the interests of offenders and victims as a 'zero sum' where anything done to benefit offenders could be criticised as 'not helping the victim' or met with demands for victims to receive some compensating benefit.

My first tasks as I saw them were to help Victim Support, led by Helen Reeves, to achieve some proper funding and recognition by government, and to work with Victim Support towards a better understanding of the issues on the part of the criminal justice and other relevant services. The police and the Crown Prosecution Service needed to show more sensitivity towards victims in the investigation and prosecution of the crimes they had experienced; the court services needed to do so in the way in which they treated victims and witnesses in court; and the Probation Service needed to do so in protecting them from unwelcome attention from their offenders while under supervision or after release from prison. All those involved changes in established assumptions and practices, and sometimes culture as well. Progress required a great deal of laborious effort on the part of Victim Support, but also active encouragement and support from the Home Office which we tried to give them.

A significant development was the Victim's Charter, first issued early in 1990. It was, unusually at that time, the result of a direct intervention by David Waddington as Home Secretary in order to balance the 'offender-oriented' proposals which were being carried forward in green and white papers and then in the Bill for the Criminal Justice Act 1991. It set out for the first time what victims were entitled to expect from the criminal justice process and its agencies. Critics within the victim support movement at first regarded it with some scepticism because it had no mechanism for enforcement and might have a limiting effect on developments that were not within the terms of the charter. In the event the charter was accepted and effective in consolidating the progress that had been made over the previous ten years and providing a foundation for further progress.

Restorative justice found its first practical expression in the mid-1980s with four pilot schemes for 'family group conferences', two of them run by the Probation Service and two by voluntary organizations. They were a new and exciting idea, but restorative conferences were difficult to arrange, and they were time-consuming and therefore expensive. The judiciary viewed them with deep suspicion as interfering with the course of justice (I had a difficult meeting when I had to justify them to Lord Justice Watkins); they were perceived as being more for the benefit of the offender than the victim; and they were ridiculed by the press ('Tell them you're sorry and they'll let you off'). There was little enthusiasm for them among academic lawyers or criminologists. It was clear that progress would be slow and laborious, and all credit is due to those who persevered and kept the subject alive so that it now beginning to find a place in the mainstream of criminal justice. See also *Chapter 12*.

Children

Most of the department's responsibilities for children had been transferred to the Department of Health in 1969. Many people regretted the change because its responsibilities for children were one of its more 'liberal' or 'humane' areas. James Callaghan in his bicentenary lecture had called it 'the brightest jewel in the Home Office crown'. The Home Office was still responsible for the criminal law, the criminal jurisdiction of the juvenile courts and the custodial treatment of those children who were sent to Prison Service establishments, but the Department of Health was now the leading department for most other children's issues.

The numbers of children under 17 sentenced to custody had increased rapidly during the 1970s, and both departments were keen to reduce them. The Department of Health funded a programme of 'intermediate treatment'—intensive, specified activities carried out in the community which could be used as a substitute to custody; Home Office ministers accepted a set of amendments which Baroness Faithfull introduced to the Bill for the Criminal Justice Act 1982 restricting the use of custodial sentences for that age group; and ministers in both departments were ready to argue for 'minimum intervention' in sentencing, often with the support of magistrates.

For most of the 1980s the system of juvenile justice and the measures the government had introduced seemed to be working well. Fewer juveniles were receiving custodial sentences,[7] and the rate of known juvenile offending was falling. A growing body of research by David Farrington and others had identified the 'risk' and 'resilience' factors which were associated with offending behaviour, all of them related to the person's situation in their family or community. It showed that most young people who get into trouble will usually grow out of crime, and that early experience of the criminal justice system, and especially of custody, was more likely to increase than to reduce the chances that they would reoffend. Intermediate treatment seemed to be successful, and with the encouragement of ministers magistrates seemed to be increasingly ready to use it as an alternative to a custodial sentence. The juvenile court in Basingstoke, where Bryan Gibson was clerk to the justices, was a 'custody free zone' for several years. There was much interest in the Scottish system of children's hearings; there was no serious attempt to replicate them in England and Wales but some features were later incorporated in the reforms of the youth courts under the Youth Justice and Criminal Evidence Act 1999. Some of us hoped that it might eventually be possible to end the use of penal custody altogether for those of school age, together with an increase in the age of criminal responsibility to 15 or 16.

What had seemed to be success during the 1980s came to be seen as failure during the 1990s. The shock of James Bulger's death in 1993, killed by children who were only eleven years old, and the simultaneous campaign by the police who claimed that parts of the country were overrun by young people who were out of control, had a deep effect on public feeling to which ministers felt they had to respond. The Labour Party, where Tony Blair had replaced Roy Hattersley as shadow Home Secretary, saw it as an opportunity to be more assertive criticising the government. Whether juvenile offending had actually been falling during the 1980s, or whether the fall in known juvenile offending was because no one bothered to report or record it, has never been

---

7.   The number aged 14 and under 17 fell from 7,300 in 1982 to 1,200 in 1990; the number aged 17 and under 21 fell from 23,200 to 14,100,

fully explained. Whether we were too complacent, and failed to notice the things we did not want to see, is hard to judge. It may be that 'minimum intervention', intended to mean that criminal proceedings and especially custody should be used sparingly, was understood as implying that nothing much needed be done at all, although that had never been the intention. We recognised that early intervention to stabilise and strengthen families and to promote the 'resistance factors' were important—that would have been part of the purpose of 'Action for Youth'—but the government did not see it as a priority, or perhaps rightly as the responsibility of the Home Office or of criminal justice.

Drugs

The abuse of drugs did not have a high political profile in 1982. Policy in Great Britain had traditionally, and was still, based primarily on treatment, education and interdiction—preventing drugs from entering the country. The British approach had gained the country a high international reputation. Dangerous drugs were controlled, possession and supply were criminal offences and the law was enforced, but law and its enforcement were not the primary means of dealing with abuse and addiction. They were seen as problems to be prevented, treated and managed, but not as ones that could realistically be eradicated. Bing Spear, the Home Office chief inspector, represented that point of view and was highly respected in this country and abroad.[8]. The 'war on drugs' had not yet been declared.

The situation changed rapidly during the early-1980s. The increasing scale on which people, especially young people, were abusing drugs and the tragic results and publicity which sometimes followed led to a much greater degree of public awareness and concern. Combined with international pressure, especially from the United States, it created a demand for stronger enforcement to which the police were happy to respond and which ministers could not resist without doing political damage to themselves. Apart from the conflict between law enforcement and prevention and treatment, there was tension between HM Customs and Excise, whose duty was to prevent the drugs from entering the country, and the police who wanted to allow drugs

---

8.   For an appreciation, see Alan Travis, *Guardian*, 11 September, 2002, accessible at http://www.guardian.co.uk/society/2002/sep/11/drugsandalcohol.guardiansocietysupplement

to 'run' so that they could arrest and prosecute the traffickers. There was also a difference of culture between HM Customs and Excise which was a centralised government department staffed by civil servants accountable to ministers, and operationally independent police forces and police officers. Relations between the two services were for a time extremely difficult and I tried, with limited success, to bring about a better understanding. I had some sympathy with Customs, and especially with the view that it would be better to keep drugs out of the country altogether, so far as that was possible, than to risk drugs going into circulation if a police operation failed, but high profile police operations had an obvious political attraction.

Helped by polished presentations by the police to ministers, judges and conferences of various kinds, drug abuse came to be seen as primarily a matter of supply and possession, to be dealt with as crimes like any other, and less as a social and public health problem to be dealt with by education and treatment. I did my best to emphasise treatment and education whenever I had the opportunity, but the strategy which the government published in 1985[9] emphasised international cooperation to limit the cultivation of drugs in other countries; increasing the number and improving the efficiency of Customs and Excise staff; strengthening police drug squads; increasing penalties; and controlling the storage and distribution of licit drugs. I thought that the concentration on control and enforcement was misguided and our priorities mistaken, but the momentum had become impossible to resist. In other areas of policy I felt that we had a map and a sense of direction, even if we were not sure of the destination. For drugs I felt we had neither.

Miscarriages of Justice

One of the functions about which I felt uncomfortable was the Criminal Department's responsibility for dealing with complaints of wrongful convictions. The rule was that the Home Office would not become involved unless and until the person had exhausted all their rights of appeal, and then only if there was new evidence that had not been available to the trial court or the Court of Appeal. If there seemed to be new evidence, the Home Office could ask the police to investigate it, and could then refer the case back to

9. Home Office, *Tackling Drug Misuse: A Summary of the Government's Strategy,* London: Home Office, 1985.

the Court of Appeal if the conviction seemed unsafe. Very exceptionally, the Royal Prerogative of Mercy could be invoked to grant a 'free pardon'. But reinvestigations were expensive, and the police would not always take them seriously if they thought the case was frivolous or trivial, or if the person had other convictions which were not in dispute. The situation was deeply unfair and was subject to bitter and too often justified criticism, especially from Tom Sargent as secretary of JUSTICE.

There were several dramatic and notorious cases during the 1980s and 1990s when the Court of Appeal set aside convictions as being unsafe, especially in cases of Irish terrorism (the Birmingham Six, the Guildford Four and the Maguire Seven), but in others as well. The defendants ought not to have been convicted in the first place, and it was inexcusable that it should have taken so many years to overturn their convictions once the doubts had emerged. Douglas Hurd's decision to refer the Birmingham Six to the Court of Appeal in 1988 was exceptionally difficult in the circumstances of the time, and it was one where he saw that public duty had to override any political considerations there might be.

Those cases led to the appointment of the Royal Commission on Criminal Justice and to the establishment of the Criminal Cases Review Authority which was set up in 1995 following the Royal Commission's report.[10] It was perhaps the most valuable outcome of the Royal Commission, whose terms of reference placed it firmly in the developing culture of effectiveness and efficiency and whose report sometimes read as if it were a consultants' management review. They also placed the conviction of those who are guilty in front of the acquittal of those who are innocent. They were a long way from Blackstone's dictum that 'It is better that ten guilty persons escape than one innocent suffers', and from the attitudes of the Home Office when I first joined the department.

---

10.   Royal Commission on Criminal Justice *Report*, Cm 2263, London: HMSO, 1993.

CHAPTER 9

Towards the Criminal Justice Act 1991

A Programme for a New Parliament

The Conservative government's re-election to office after the general election in 1987, with Douglas Hurd's return to the Home Office as Home Secretary and the appointment of John Patten and Douglas Hogg as ministers of state, promised a period of political stability in which it would be possible to take a strategic view of criminal justice and the country's response to crime extending over the full period of the Parliament. It did not mark a turning point, but rather a reaffirmation and of the direction in which the government had been moving for the previous few years. The Conservative party's manifesto had promised few new criminal justice measures, and emphasised that the origins of crime lie deep in society and cannot be tackled successfully by government alone. Communities must play their part and there would be a new voluntary organization — Crime Concern — to help them. There were no further distractions such as attempts to restore the death penalty or demands for new eye-catching forms of punishment such as the tougher regimes in detention centres.

Douglas Hurd did not see himself as a penal reformer but as a pragmatist, resolving what he called 'muddles', making things work better, and doing so with a settled sense of direction and purpose. The foundations had already been laid in the work we had already begun on preventing and reducing crime, and on minorities and victims, and there was still unfinished business — to continue the rationalisation of criminal justice legislation, to make further progress towards stabilising the prison population and to integrate the Crown Prosecution Service more closely into the machinery of government.

The most serious strategic issues in criminal justice were still those of sentencing and the prison population. Reviewing the situation after the government had returned to office, ministers saw how sentencing had become more severe since 1979, and especially since 1983–84,000 custodial sentences had been passed in 1985 compared with 63,000 in 1979, and the proportion of custodial sentences passed by the Crown Court had risen to 55% in 1985 from 52% in 1983. There had been a surge in the prison population which rose from 43,300 in 1984 to almost 51,000 in July 1987, and the projections showed that it might reach 54,000 by 1991. Northeye Prison had been burnt to the ground in a disturbance during the previous year. New prisons were being built, but the projected shortfall in accommodation was 6,800 places.

Ministers took an immediate decision to increase remission from one third to one half of the sentence, so reducing the population by about 3,000 and resolving the situation in the short term. It was an operational necessity at the time, and it did not attract the criticism that it would have done when the political temperature and public concern about crime had increased a few years later. Even so, for prisoners to be routinely released at the half-way point in their sentences created a problem of perception and confidence, and a justifiable demand for 'truth in sentencing', which continue to this day. The change also drew attention to the problem that although remission was supposed to be 'earned', that meant only that the prisoner had to stay out of trouble. Prisons did not have the capacity to provide opportunities for more positive achievement in work, education or service to the community for more than a minority of prisoners.

The Options Available

Soon after the general election Douglas Hurd held a meeting at Leeds Castle with his ministerial team and senior officials to review the main issues which would face the Home Office during the period of the new Parliament. It covered some of the same ground as the seminars which Brian Cubbon had arranged five years before, but from a more political perspective and with the full team of ministers taking part. The discussion covered the whole range of Home Office business, including policing, immigration and broadcasting. On criminal justice it confirmed the importance of crime prevention and the need to engage communities and the public, and there was some inconclusive discussion on the scope for requiring parents to take more responsibility for the behaviour of their children, but the critical issues were prisons and sentencing. John Patten presented the argument that the government might allow the prison population to rise and create whatever capacity was needed to contain the increase, and to take credit for doing so as part of a more robust response to crime. Against that Lord Caithness, the minister for prisons, pointed out that the rate at which the population was increasing, and would continue to increase if it followed the projections, might cause it to become out of control before enough new capacity could be provided.

At a subsequent meeting to review the options and take decisions, we put three alternatives to ministers which were to

- take no special position on sentencing and continue to handle situations as they arose;
- expand prison capacity as necessary to match public and judicial demand for more severe sentencing; or
- exert some downward pressure on the rise in the prison population, and therefore on the sentencing of those not regarded as a threat to society.

My own and my colleagues' preference was for the third, but I was concerned that we should present the choices and their implications as dispassionately as possible and without a recommendation of our own on the choice to be made between them. Some of my colleagues thought it unwise to present the issues in such an open-ended fashion, but I did not want the decision to come to be seen as a matter of cost or expediency from which ministers would depart when circumstances became more favourable, still less as a one which civil servants could be said to have somehow forced on ministers. I wanted it to be a clear and principled political decision, which ministers had taken for themselves and which they would be prepared to defend over a period of time.

Ministers decided on the third option, as I had hoped. The range of measures that might be taken to reduce the prison population was already well-known — earlier release, including release on parole; guidance from judgements in the Court of Appeal; reductions in maximum sentences; greater use of community sentences to replace imprisonment; increased use of fines; and statutory restrictions on the use of imprisonment. There was no more mileage to be obtained from earlier release, and although judgements by the Court of Appeal had been helpful in the past (see *Chapter 5*) they were unlikely have a significant effect, even if that court were to agree. Reductions in maximum sentences might have some symbolic effect but were unlikely to have any direct or immediate impact because the sentences which courts actually imposed were usually well below the statutory maximum. We saw scope for persuading courts to make more use of community sentences in preference to imprisonment,[1] but more by tightening up their administration and making them more 'demanding' in order to improve their rehabilitative effect than by making the experience deliberately more unpleasant or humiliating. If that were done, there would be a risk that more offenders would breach the conditions of their orders and go to prison, but many probation officers, some of my colleagues and I also saw objections of principle.

We were especially concerned about the decline in the courts' use of the fine, which had been identified as an issue in Brian Cubbon's seminars in 1982. Because of the difficulty of imposing 'realistic' fines on people with limited means, for example single parents and those living on benefits, courts had been making probation and community service orders instead. By doing so they not only added to the workload and costs of the Probation Service, but they also affected prisons because of the greater likelihood of custody if the person breached the order or committed a further offence. To deal with the difficulty we had devised a scheme for 'day' or 'unit' fines, where the amount would be expressed in 'units' and then translated into cash terms by reference to the person's means. It had been successfully tested in four magistrates' courts, it was already being adopted more widely, and we thought it could now be extended nationally and placed on a statutory basis.[2]

In 1980 a report by Justice[3] had proposed a 'middle' system of law, with a distinction between 'crimes' and 'contraventions'. A range of criminal offences would be taken out of the criminal process and dealt with as 'contraventions', being enforced administratively by financial penalties or orders to carry out certain works or pay compensation for damage or loss. Penalties

---

1. We avoided using the term 'alternatives' to custody, which implied that imprisonment was the norm and 'alternatives' has to be justified as an exception to it.
2. Under the system that was proposed, the seriousness of an offence would be assessed in units on a scale from one to 50. This number would then be multiplied by the offender's own disposable weekly income to create the unit fine. The intentions included greater fairness, a potential for consistency, a better structure for judicial decision-making and more openness. Unit fines would thus be linked directly to means, and courts might be more ready to impose fines of offenders of limited means who would not be able to pay a fine levied at the existing normal rate. The principle would be one of 'equal sacrifice' or 'equal impact'.
3. JUSTICE, *Breaking the Rules,* London: JUSTICE, 1980.

would not include loss of liberty, and the person would not incur a conviction or criminal record. Part of the reasoning was to reduce what JUSTICE even then saw as the unnecessary proliferation of criminal offences, but the proposal would also have had the effect of reducing the use of imprisonment. Louk Hulsman in The Netherlands put forward a similar proposal at about the same time.[4] I thought it was in many ways an attractive proposal, but the apparatus needed for a new and parallel system of enforcement and adjudication would have been expensive, and the practical benefits would have been speculative and long-term. The government's view was that more certain progress could made by extending the use of fixed penalties and police cautions. No connection was made with restorative justice, which was still almost unknown.

Moving Towards Legislation

Ministers agreed that measures of that kind, although useful in themselves, would not be enough and legislation was needed on the sentencing framework itself. The Bill for the Criminal Justice Act 1988 was already before Parliament, with further restrictions on the custodial sentencing of young people extending those which had already been included in the Criminal Justice Act 1982, but we did not expect it to have a significant effect on the prison population as a whole.

The legislative framework for sentencing was still relatively straightforward. The special sentences of preventive detention, corrective training and borstal training had been abolished over the years and the sentence of detention in a detention centre would be abolished by the 1988 Act; the life sentence for murder was the only sentence which courts were statutorily required to impose. Apart from the restrictions on the custodial sentencing of young people introduced by the Criminal Justice Act 1982 and in due course 1988, the Crown Court had more or less unlimited discretion within the statutory maximum for the particular offence. The courts were guided by the precedents set by previous judgements, brought together in David Thomas's

---

4. Louk Hulsman, 'Penal Reform in the Netherlands: Part 2 — Criteria for Deciding on Alternatives to Imprisonment', *Howard Journal of Criminal Justice*, 21, 1982. Andrew Ashworth put forward a similar idea 20 years later — Andrew Ashworth, 'Is the Criminal Law a Lost Cause?', *The Law Quarterly Review*, vol 116, 225-256, 2000.

Principles of Sentencing,[5] and by the Court of Appeal's guideline judgements where they applied, but there were no clear purposes for sentencing. Judges often spoke vaguely about 'retribution, deterrence and rehabilitation', but there was no common understanding of the relationship between them or how they were to be achieved through sentencing practice. Nor were there any principles or guidance for dealing with considerations such as mitigating or aggravating circumstances; the justification for deterrent or exemplary sentences, for example when an offence was considered to be 'prevalent'; the attention to be paid to a person's previous record, including the 'repeat' offender who persistently commits minor offences and is a nuisance but not a danger to society; or the treatment of multiple offences when several offences were being tried at the same time.

Scholars including Andrew Ashworth, Roger Hood and Andrew von Hirsch had drawn attention to the resulting anomalies and inconsistencies[6] and had argued for 'proportionality' as a guiding principle—that is to say, the sentence should be proportionate to the harm which the offence had caused and the culpability of the offender. I was attracted by Andrew Ashworth's proposal for a Sentencing Council,[7] but the Lord Chief Justice had expressed his opposition to it and ministers were unwilling to take the risk of another public rift of the kind that had occurred in 1981. They were also reluctant to set up an influential public body which they would not be able to control. Experience in the United States suggested that guidelines might have the effect of 'levelling upwards' and so increase rather than reduce the general length of sentences, and although a Sentencing Council might be useful in promoting consistency and transparency it might not be effective in controlling the prison population. The proposal was set aside until the Labour government revived it in the form of a Sentencing Advisory Panel after it came into office in 1997.

We accordingly began to work towards legislation. Ministers agreed that

---

5. David Thomas, *Principles of Sentencing,* London: Heinemann, 1976. The judges regarded Dr David Thomas, Reader in Law at Cambridge, as the country's leading academic lawyer on sentencing and he was a regular and influential speaker at judicial sentencing seminars.

6. See for example Andrew Ashworth, *Sentencing and Penal Policy,* London: Weidenfeld and Nicholson, 1983. Their ideas were among those which we discussed at the discussion group described in *Chapter 5.*

7. In *Sentencing and Penal Policy,* 447-451.

we should if possible use it to resolve some of the 'muddles' in sentencing, as Douglas Hurd described them, as well as aiming to limit the use of imprisonment in order to deal with the problem of the prison population. A few weeks after the meeting at Leeds Castle, I set out some preliminary ideas in a talk to magistrates. I described the background, the issues as the Home Office saw them, the evidence from research and the experience of other countries. I explained our scepticism about the effectiveness of sentencing and the need as we saw it for a better understanding of the principles on which sentencing should be based and the place it should occupy in our arrangements for dealing with crime. I said

> One of the tragedies of the last 25 years has been the way in which prison over-crowding has come to dominate and distort the argument about penal policy. The argument ought to have been on what scale, for what purpose and for what sort of offenders the ultimate sanction of imprisonment ought to be used. Instead it has been mostly about how we could reduce prison overcrowding and what sentencing and other devices could be introduced to achieve that result. The consequence has been that what ought to have been an argument of principle has become confused with arguments of expediency and cost, and the whole debate has become over-laid with cynicism suspicion and unhealthy recriminations between the judiciary and the executive with the Probation Service placed awkwardly between them.

I then introduced the ideas of sufficiency and proportionality—

> If the offence is serious the offender must be punished as severely, but no more severely, than justice and public confidence require. This is not of course the same as imposing a sentence which will be applauded by the local newspapers or as ensuring that the sentence will never be criticised by them. But the sentence should be one which will not leave a sense of injustice or incomprehension among those, including the offender and the victim, who know the facts of the case and the considerations and principles involved. Those may sometimes have to be carefully explained.

But I did not entirely abandon the idea of rehabilitation—

The sentence or disposal8 should, so far as possible, be one which will not increase the propensity of the offender or others to commit further offences; and it should so far as possible reinforce or at least leave intact such positive influences or opportunities as are available to him or he r. This is particularly important for the juvenile or young adult offender who may be on the threshold of a life of crime, probably becoming increasingly serious as he or she gets older, or who may be one of the much larger majority for whom offending is only an adolescent phase.

Especially for young offenders, I argued for

...the use of disposals which will so far as possible allow the offender to take advantage of such opportunities as may be available to him or her, to take personal responsibility for doing so, and to have the benefit of such positive influences as can be brought to bear on his or her situation. Those opportunities and influences are more likely to operate in the community than in custody and it follows that in those cases where the need for punishment permits a non-custodial—or I would prefer to say normal—disposal then that should be the preferred sentence. It is the task of the Home Office and of the probation service to develop these opportunities wherever we can and that is what we will be trying to do in the coming months.

Those were preliminary ideas and I was encouraged that the magistrates seemed sympathetic towards them. As work proceeded, we became more strongly convinced that the principle of proportionality provided a foundation on which to do that, and which was also consistent with much existing practice.[9] The legislation would lay down the main principles, especially those of sufficiency and proportionality but without definitions which we hoped, as it turned out unrealistically, would emerge from the courts' own jurisprudence. It would build on the provisions in the Criminal Justice Acts 1982 and 1988 to limit the use of imprisonment but without (we thought) imposing too many constraints on judges' discretion. It would also enact

8.   The word 'disposal' was used because a probation order was at that time not a sentence but an alternative to it.
9.   The Court of Appeal had given a helpful judgement in *R v Queen* (1981) 3 Cr App R (S) 245, where it claimed that persistence should be dealt with not as an aggravating factor but by progressive loss of mitigation.

a system of unit fines, establish criteria for the use of custody, community sentences and fines, and symbolically reduce the maximum sentence for non-domestic burglary. To emphasise that probation was a punishment, the probation order would become a sentence of the court and not an alternative to it. The government would make clear that the legislation was part of a wider programme to improve the quality of justice, including for victims and minorities, and to reduce crime by whatever measures were available.

Consultation and Discussion, Criminal Justice Conferences

Sir Clive Whitmore succeeded Sir Brian Cubbon as Permanent Secretary in 1988 and gave his full support to what we were doing. The government's proposals were published, first in the green paper *Punishment, Custody and the Community*,[10] and then in the white papers *Crime, Justice and Protecting the Public*[11] on the proposed structure for sentencing, and *Supervision and Punishment in the Community*[12] on the organization and practice of the Probation Service. I was pleased that a committee set up by JUSTICE and composed of distinguished judges and lawyers had put forward similar proposals in a report[13] which coincided with the green paper.

The green paper provided the basis for a conference at Ditchley Park in September 1989 which brought together the most senior figures in criminal justice in England and Wales, including the Home Secretary, the Lord Chancellor, the Attorney General, the Lord Chief and Deputy Lord Chief Justice, the Chairman of the Magistrates' Association, the Director of Public Prosecutions and the leaders of the criminal justice services. Its purpose was to enable minister to explain the situation as they saw it and the options they were considering, emphasising that their two main aims were to establish the principles of sufficiency and proportionality in sentencing and to reinforce the links between offenders and society. Ministers were not seeking any formal agreement to the proposals, but they hoped for and I think achieved a friendly and constructive discussion and what seemed to be a sympathetic reaction to what they were trying to do. There may have been some wishful

10. Home Office, *Punishment, Custody and the Community* (Cm 424), London: HMSO, 1988.
11. Home Office, *Crime, Justice and Protecting the Public* (Cm 965), London: HMSO, 1990.
12. Home Office, *Supervision and Punishment in the Community: A Framework for Action* (Cm 966), London: HMSO, 1990.
13. JUSTICE, *Sentencing: A Way Ahead*, London: JUSTICE, 1989.

thinking, and the judges' goodwill may have been mistaken for agreement to the policy, but ministers were sufficiently encouraged to proceed to the white paper *Crime, Justice and Protecting the Public* which followed early in 1990 and the to the Bill for the Criminal Justice Act 1991, itself.

The conference at Ditchley was followed by a series of residential national and more local conferences , with similar objectives, where people from across the criminal justice system could meet and discuss the issues that were live at the time, and others which might not be receiving much attention but which we wanted to expose for debate. National conferences extended over five days; regional conferences were at a weekend. Reports were written and circulated, and the conferences were individually evaluated and periodically reviewed. The conferences were generally and sometimes enthusiastically appreciated by those who took part, even though they took up quite a lot of people's time. We tried to make sure that there was a reasonable balance between the number of men and women taking part and some representation from minority groups, and at national conferences a contribution from another European country whenever possible. Subjects discussed covered not only the prospective legislation on sentencing, but also issues of race and gender; the treatment of victims, including the humiliating treatment of victims of rape when they are called as witnesses — one of the first occasions when the issue was treated seriously; the often poor quality of the representation provided for children appearing in court; and management issues of various kinds, such as the often hidden problem of depression among police and prison officers. The conferences helped to improve the participants' and our own awareness of issues and ideas, and contributed to a better understanding between the different parts of the system including the Home Office itself.

The Criminal Justice Act 1991

I was conscious that the programme we had gradually built up was politically precarious, especially after Douglas Hurd moved to become Foreign Secretary soon after the Ditchley conference, to be succeeded by David Waddington. We had been fortunate that the political confrontations which had taken place in other areas of government during Mrs Thatcher's administration had not extended to criminal justice, and the Labour party and its Labour Party Campaign for Criminal Justice had broadly supported what the government

was doing. Public and political opinion was becoming more polarised, with
the prospect of a general election within the next 18 months, but David
Waddington nevertheless continued Hurd's policies during his own period
as Home Secretary, and the Bill for the Criminal Justice Act 1991 was duly
introduced and completed its passage through Parliament. The Act is most
often remembered for its sentencing provisions, but it also dealt with other
subjects — the reorganization of parole following the Carlisle Committee's
review, children's evidence, the administration of sentences of life imprisonment, the electronic monitoring of offenders, the responsibilities of parents,
the separation of the family and criminal jurisdictions of the magistrates'
courts, various measures intended to improve efficiency and effectiveness,
and especially the contracting-out of prisons and prison escorts to which I
return in *Chapter 10*. They had different origins — the Carlisle committee's
report on parole, the report of an advisory group on children's evidence,
judgements of the European Court of Human Rights, discussions with the
judiciary, and the department's own ideas. Those on electronic monitoring,
the responsibilities of parents and contracting-out were more politically
driven, but only the last was seriously contested in party political terms.[14]

The criticisms of the sentencing provisions related principally to unit
fines and those intended to give force to the principle of proportionality.
Although unit fines had been successfully tested before the Act came into
effect, a decision had been taken to increase the general level of fines to take
account of inflation and the carefully calculated ratios between unit fines
and the amounts to be paid were consequently thrown out of gear and some
absurdly heavy fines were (unnecessarily and perhaps provocatively) imposed
as a result. The principle of unit fines also attracted public criticism because
they were seen as penalising, or 'taxing' those who were required to pay the
full amount. Rather than correct the scheme, the home Secretary (then
Kenneth Clarke) decided to abandon it altogether.

As to proportionality, we had decided that it was too difficult to attempt
a statutory definition, but instead the Act specified that a court should not

---

14. See Lord Windlesham, *Responses to Crime*, Vol 2, *Penal Policy in the Making*, Oxford: Clarendon Press, 1993, chapter for a more detailed discussion, including the disagreement between
the House of Lords and the House of Commons over an amendment to abolish the mandatory life sentence for murder.

regard an offence as more serious by reason of any previous convictions the offender might have, or his (or her) failure to respond to previous sentences; and that, when several offences were being dealt with together, the sentence should be based on the gravity of the most serious offence, or that offence and one other. David Thomas criticised those provisions as pointless and unnecessary, refusing to accept either the principle of proportionality or the weakness of deterrence and rehabilitation as objectives of sentencing. They also attracted vehement criticism from the new Lord Chief Justice, Lord Taylor,[15] who described the Act as an 'ill-fitting straightjacket'. In response to those, and to political reactions more generally, the Act was amended to abolish unit fines and to remove both those provisions. The amendments were hurriedly made by late additions to the Bill for the Criminal Justice Act 1993. The judges' criticisms of the legislation were then largely resolved. The principle of proportionality itself remained but the Court of Appeal had undermined it in a series of judgements issued at the end of 1992,[16] which among other things reintroduced deterrence and public opinion as factors which sentencers should consider.

David Thomas had a major influence on the judges' attitude to the Bill and their reaction to the Act. They and many magistrates held him in high regard and his view that neither government nor Parliament has any business to interfere with sentencing was naturally attractive to them. He was extremely knowledgeable, he had frequent meetings with senior judges at the Judicial Studies Board and was a regular speaker at the board's sentencing seminars. It may be a pity that more attention was not paid to his criticisms, but his opposition to the whole basis of the Act was so implacable that constructive dialogue seemed impossible. It would have been possible for the provisions relating to previous convictions and related offences not to have been included in the first place, leaving only the principle of proportionality on the face of the Bill, or they might have been amended during its passage. They were however seen as necessary for the objectives which the Bill was intended to achieve, and the hope and expectation was that once the Act was in place the judges would acclimatise themselves to it. That hope was not realised, but no change which might have been considered would

---

15.   Lord Lane, who had been present at Ditchley, had by then retired.
16.   Especially in *Cunningham* 14 Cr App R (S) 444.

have made any difference to the wider reactions and the change of political direction which followed from 1993 onwards.

In October, 1990, I gave a talk to a conference of European and Canadian judges at Breda in The Netherlands in which I tried to give an account of what we had been doing in England and Wales, put it in perspective, and describe what I saw as the prospects for the future. After describing the process which led up to the Bill and the arguments we had considered, I said

> We still have a long way to go. The enactment of legislation is only the first and not necessarily the most important part of a difficult programme which still lies ahead. There is an argument that legislation on sentencing principles and community sentences is not needed at all. It is said, for example, that more coherent sentencing principles can if necessary be developed through the courts' own jurisprudence; and that stronger forms of community sentence can be developed administratively through changes in Probation Service practice. The Government's view is that the judiciary and the probation service are not by nature reforming institutions, and that neither more coherent sentencing nor stronger community sentences will come about without the stimulus and authority of legislation.

> Even so, the way in which the courts develop their own jurisprudence, and the way in which the probation service develops its own professional practice and management skills, will still be crucial to the programme's success. A major programme of training will be needed for judges and magistrates, matched by a similar programme for the probation service, if the changes are to be brought into effect as intended, and if they are to carry the confidence and collective commitment that will be required. The situation is at present quite precarious—recoded crime is again increasing, and some commentators are beginning to claim, without any real evidence, that the increase is because not enough people are being locked up. An alternative explanation that the increase is a result of the Government's social and economic policies is not one which the Government finds any easier to accept. The reasons and the facts themselves are, of course, a good deal more complex, but the danger of a punitive reaction, especially as we approach another General Election, is a factor which has to be taken seriously into account.

Neither Douglas Hurd nor I originally saw the reforms of sentencing as the radical new departure that was sometimes claimed afterwards. We saw them more as providing a practical legislative framework in which courts would come to make less use of imprisonment, but some of the anomalies in sentencing would also be removed, some principles and especially the principle of proportionality would be reinforced, and sentencing would become more explicable and consistent. It was a pity that reducing the use of imprisonment came to be seen as their only purpose, and that the principle of proportionality, or 'just deserts' as it was called in the white paper (unfortunately misspelt), came to be dismissed as 'academic theory', or even as 'foreign academic theory'.[17]

The Sentencing Provisions in Retrospect

Legislation of the 1980s also established precedents for legislative interference in sentencing, at first to reduce the use of custody or imprisonment but later for broader political and declaratory purposes — to 'send a message'. As a gesture to public opinion but against its own principles, the Criminal Justice Act 1991 itself included a provision (section 2(2)(b)) which allowed disproportionately long sentences for serious sexual or violent offences, a distinction which gathered momentum later. The Labour government went further in calling for 'progression' in sentencing (every previous conviction should be treated as an aggravating factor),[18] and for offenders to be treated 'for who they are and not for what they have done'.[19] The principle of proportionality remains in section 143 of the Criminal Justice Act 2003, which requires the court to 'consider the offender's culpability in committing the offence and any harm which the offence caused...', but it has become

---

17. In his article 'The Fall of the Platonic Guardians', Ian Loader reports comments made in interviews which referred to the 'perceived shifts in the nature and use of expertise' and to '... the altered role and reduced standing of Home Office civil servants — what one may call the eclipse of "dedicated Home Office men". Some referred in specific terms ...to the "enormous sense of disillusion" felt by ministers towards the Home Office in the aftermath of its successful attempt to enshrine "the justice model" in the 1991 Criminal Justice Act: "The Faulkner bill, if you like, sewed iron into the soul, both of Tories and Labour, about the Home Office as an institution which couldn't be trusted" (retired Home Office civil servant)'. Ian Loader 'Fall of the Platonic Guardians: Liberalism, Criminology and Political Responses to Crime in England and Wales', *British Journal of Criminology* (2006), 46, 561-586.

18. Section 143(2) of the Criminal Justice Act 2003.

19. Tony Blair, *A New Consensus on Law and Order.* Speech on the Government's 5-Year Strategy for Crime, 2004.

progressively diluted as other considerations have been introduced as aggravating factors (for example previous convictions) or relevant considerations (such as deterrence or prevalence), and by the introduction of mandatory minimum sentences. The Criminal Justice Act 2003 introduced statutory purposes for sentencing,[20] but the 'muddles' which we tried to resolve in the Criminal Justice Act 1991 still for the most part remain.[21]

An unanswered question is whether, if the aim was to reduce and then to limit the prison population, the 1991 Act was really needed at all. The courts' use of imprisonment was falling between 1989 and 1992, before the Act had been passed and even before the Bill had been published. Perhaps the fall was because the courts were anticipating the Act and would have reverted to more punitive practices if the Act had not been in prospect. Or perhaps they were responding to a temporary climate of political and possibly public opinion in which community sentences had become more acceptable for cases where imprisonment would previously have been imposed. However that may be, the history of legislative attempts to structure sentencing for instrumental or declaratory purposes has not been encouraging. No one can doubt Parliament's right to make them, but its wisdom when it has done so has been more open to question.

I now wonder if Parliament should in general confine itself to its traditional role of setting the maximum penalty for the various offences and the rules on eligibility for release, and leave the courts to maintain consistency of practice and approach within a framework of sentencing guidelines drawn up by an independent but representative guidelines council, similar to the Sentencing Council that has now been established. The guidelines would have regard to public feeling but government would not try to influence sentencing directly and sentencing would not be a party political issue. The composition of the council, its method of appointment and its procedures for consultation—to take account of public feeling and opinion, but not in a context of emotional reactions to particular events or party politics—should be such as to give its work legitimacy and authority and governments should

---

20. In Section 142(1)—namely, punishment; the reduction of crime, including by deterrence; reform and rehabilitation; protection of the public; and reparation.
21. See Andrew Ashworth, *Sentencing and Criminal Justice,* 5th edition, Cambridge University Press, 2010, chapters 3–6.

have enough confidence in the it and the judiciary to stand back from the council's work. The problem of sentencing and prison capacity would be discussed and so far as possible resolved in places such as the national forum and local committees which the Woolf report recommended (see below), in a context where there was mutual understanding and respect between government and the judiciary.

Perhaps the most damaging criticism of the policies we followed during the 1980s has been that the attempts to limit the use of imprisonment caused the rise in crime which continued through the 1980s and until the mid-1990s, and that the increase in imprisonment from 1993 onwards caused the fall in crime which then followed. During the 1990s Home Office officials were criticised for being defeatist about the rise in crime. We were sceptical about the effectiveness of sentencing in reducing crime, but I do not think we were defeatist about crime itself and we put a lot of effort into promoting other ways of preventing it and reducing the damage it causes. Governments of both parties have since then accepted, sometimes reluctantly, the evidence that changes in rates of imprisonment have only a marginal effect on rates of crime.[22] The reasons for the fall which began in 1995 are uncertain and complicated, but I would like to think that the work we had begun on crime prevention made a contribution. So, probably, did the loss of the market for easily carried, high-value, stolen goods—although others such as ipads, ipods and iphones have taken their place, and there are other kinds of crime—cybercrime, credit card fraud, illegal downloading—which may never be reported or recorded.

Some writers have argued that the rise in crime during the 1980s can be attributed, at least in part, to the Thatcher government's social and economic policies and to increasing inequality and the consumer culture (although we would not have dared to argue that ourselves). There was research also which connected changes in rates of crime with changes in rates of economic activity, showing that property crime increases but violent crime falls during periods of decreasing economic activity. The Labour government's policies for

---

22. See for example, among recent publications, Ministry of Justice, *Green Paper Evidence Report—Breaking the Cycle: Effective Punishment, Rehabilitation and Sentencing of Offenders*, London: Ministry of Justice, 2010, 5.64: 'to date there has been no clear consensus from criminologists and commentators about whether there is an incapacitation effect at all, and if so, its scale'.

reducing poverty, for schemes such as Sure Start and its spending on health and education may have helped to sustain the fall after 1997. All those theories would however have predicted a sharp rise in crime after the financial crisis in 2008 and during the period of austerity which followed. That has not so far occurred, but it is too soon to draw firm conclusions, and there is still no clear or unqualified answer to the question 'what causes crime?' or—as criminologists would prefer—'Why and when do people commit crime?'

It remains an interesting thought that the only prime minister to have presided over a government that was seriously committed to reducing the use of imprisonment was Margaret Thatcher.

Strangeways and the Woolf Report

In April 1990 the Prison Service suffered the most serious disturbances by prisoners that it had seen for very many years, especially at Strangeways Prison in Manchester but at other prisons as well. The subsequent report by Lord Justice Woolf[23] (as he then was) recommended a number of improvements in prison conditions and management, and carried forward some of the ideas which I had tried to promote both recently and several years before. I was not directly involved either in dealing with the disturbances or with Lord Justice Woolf's inquiry, but I was able to have some discussion with him about the content and structure of his report, and I had worked closely with his advisors Gordon Lakes, Rod Morgan and Mary Tuck in the past (Rod Morgan and Mary Tuck had been members of the discussion group mentioned in *Chapter 5*).

Several of the report's recommendations carried forward work which we had begun in the 1970s and which had been continued subsequently. Examples are

- 'closer cooperation between the different parts of the criminal justice system', and for 'a national forum and local committees';
- 'better prospects for prisoners to maintain their links with families and the community through more visits and home leaves and through being located in community prisons as near to their homes as possible'; and

---

23. Lord Justice Woolf, *Report of an Inquiry into the Prison Disturbances of April 1990*, Cmnd 1456, London: HMSO 1991.

- the theme of 'justice in prisons' and specifically 'improved standards of justice within prisons involving the giving of reasons to a prisoner for any decision which materially and adversely affects him; a grievance procedure and disciplinary proceedings which ensure that the Governor deals with most matters under his present powers; relieving Boards of Visitors of their adjudicatory role; and providing for final access to an independent Complaints Adjudicator'.

The government accepted most of the recommendations in the report,[24] but they were then overlaid by the new emphasis on prison security which followed from the Lygo, Woodcock and Learmont inquiries into failures of security; by the appointment of Derek Lewis, an 'outsider' from the television industry, as director general and his subsequent dismissal; and the greater 'austerity' in prison regimes which Michael Howard demanded as Home Secretary.[25] Conditions in prisons and their safety and management were progressively improved in the years which followed, especially after Richard Tilt succeeded Derek Lewis as director general in 1995.

A Centre for Criminal Justice?

One of the ideas which emerged from the discussion group described in *Chapter 5* was for an institute or centre for criminal justice. I had in mind an institution at arm's length from government, partly funded by government and partly by one of the foundations, with access to ministers and able to undertake commissions from them, but independent of government in the studies it could pursue and the ideas it could express. It would be a college for future leaders of the criminal justice services and perhaps the judiciary, a clearing house for ideas, and a 'think tank' for making or examining proposals for new departures in policy and practice. Such a centre might help to fill the gap in policy advice that had been left when the Advisory Council on the Penal System had been abolished. Models for different aspects of what such an institution might do included the Top Management Programme

24. Home Office, *Custody, Care and Justice: The Way Ahead for the Prison Service in England and Wales*, Cmnd 1647, London: HMSO, 1991.
25. See, among other sources, Ian Dunbar's and Anthony Langdon's *Tough Justice: Sentencing and Penal Policies in the 1990s*, London: Blackstone, 1998.

for senior public servants and managers from the private sector, the Senior Course in Criminology at the Cambridge Institute of Criminology, the staff colleges for the armed forces, the Civil Service College, and at later points in time the Centre for Policy and Management Studies and the Institute for Government. Judges were themselves interested in the idea of a judicial college, which might have been associated with it.

Those ideas would have had to be refined and put in much better order before an institute or centre could actually be established, and the need for it and the benefits it would bring would have be more clearly demonstrated. It would have needed a clear focus and a well understood mandate, and it is unlikely that all those aspirations could have been realised by the creation of a single institution. Douglas Hurd agreed that work to prepare proposals could be carried forward, without any commitment to the outcome, and I hoped that experience with the national and regional conferences, mentioned in the previous chapter, might enable us to develop a more detailed and realistic specification. We drafted a framework document for the centre to be set up as an executive agency and the Treasury were quite enthusiastic, but I realised that it would have needed sustained ministerial interest and commitment to keep it alive, and it would be difficult to reconcile those with the independence needed for professional and academic credibility. It would have required a degree of confidence between ministers and those running the institution which seemed feasible in the 1980s but it would probably not have been possible later. I was disappointed but not surprised when ministers decided not to proceed with it (Kenneth Baker was by then Home Secretary).

I still believe that an institution on those lines could have played a useful and probably unique role, if it could have been funded and sustained. The issues arising from it go to the heart of questions about the kinds of institutions necessary to support developments in public policy and public services. Those questions have been discussed for much of the last 50 years. Different governments have sought different solutions, with different motives and varying degrees of success—the formation of special units in the Cabinet Office; the establishment of colleges, centres and institutes; the proliferation of politically aligned think-tanks. The search continues today.[26]

---

26. See for example Catherine Haddon, *Reforming the Civil Service — the Centre for Policy and Management Studies,* London: Institute for Government, 2012.

CHAPTER 10

The Home Office as an Organization

In October 1990 I moved to the post of Principal Establishment Officer, with responsibility for human resources (then called personnel management) and departmental services and organization. Both were centralised functions carried out by the Establishments Department for the Home Office as a whole. Quite small changes in organization or equipment — creating an extra post, regrading an existing post, a new typewriter — needed central approval. Many of the staff were long-serving 'establishment officers', who conscientiously did their best for the Home Office and their colleagues within the rules laid down by the Treasury and the Civil Service Department,[1] although other parts of the Home Office sometimes thought that 'Estabs' was secretive, remote and obstructive. Most 'Estabs' business was conducted smoothly and without serious problems: there were good relations between the Official Side and the Staff, later Trade Union, Side of the Home Office Whitley Council (I had previously sat on the Staff Side as treasurer and then secretary of the Home Office branch of the First Division Association), and the occasional disputes were handled with good sense on both sides. Pay was negotiated nationally by the Treasury except for that of prison officers.

I had served two previous tours in the Establishments Department, in 1974-1975 and briefly in 1977. The first was to the division responsible for the personnel management of specialist of professional staff, of whom there were several different kinds — forensic scientists, researchers in the Research Unit, lawyers, scientists, engineers in the various units serving the police, and academic staff at the Police College. Many felt isolated, and across the Civil Service as a whole there was concern that specialists were effectively excluded from the most senior positions. I made a point of meeting staff and of doing so on their own ground, visiting sites such as forensic science laboratories, wireless depots and the Police College at Bramshill, and encouraged

---

1. The central management of the Civil Service was transferred from the Treasury to a new Civil Service Department in 1968. The Department was later abolished by Margaret Thatcher.

colleagues to do the same. I reorganized the division on a 'client' rather than a functional basis so that staff would come to identify themselves and get to know their own 'clients' instead of specialising impersonally in particular functions or processes. I tried to develop a wider range of career opportunities for specialists through transfers to other departments or to the administrative grades through the Civil Service-wide Senior Professional Administrative Training Scheme, but I found that most professional staff preferred to develop their careers within the own discipline or specialism and to look outside the Civil Service for opportunities rather than move to work for which they had no particular appetite or in some cases aptitude.

Staff Reporting and Performance-Related Pay

I was particularly concerned about the quality of staff reporting and staff appraisal, across the Home Office as a whole. Many staff reports were bland and complacent, and very few managers discussed them seriously with the staff about whom they were written. The process was generally disliked by both parties. Managers mostly objected to 'open' reporting for fear that reports would be even less frank if staff were allowed to read them and some, usually older, staff may have preferred not to confront colleagues with criticisms of their work or to be confronted by them. In an effort to improve reporting standards across the Civil Service as a whole, the Civil Service Department had designed a system of Job Appraisal Review, to which the Staff Side objected because of what they thought was its authoritarian, top-down style and its patronising tone. Managers had no enthusiasm for it either. I devised an alternative form of 'job discussions', with opportunities for both parties to exchange views and advice in a mutual effort to improve performance, but the Home Office was not yet ready for the change of culture that it required.

Subsequently, as Principal Establishment Officer, it fell to me to carry forward the introduction of performance-related pay. None of my colleagues had any enthusiasm for it,[2] and I personally found it insulting. The arrangements for staff appraisal had been improved but I still I did not have enough confidence in them to feel sure that we could devise a fair and objective system. Different colleagues would see people's performance in different ways and take different considerations into account. Anyone's performance

---

2.   One of them commented that 'gentlemen don't take tips'.

was likely to depend on the support of colleagues, and also very often on circumstances such as the Department's relationships with other organizations, and what a person achieved could well be seen differently by different people and at different times. The closer a civil servant worked with ministers the greater the chance that they would be judged by the impression they might create and the convenience of the advice they gave. The incentive of performance related pay brings with it the temptation to manipulate the system in ways which may not be in the public interest. We set up the best arrangements we could according to the rules, but I would at least have preferred the funds available for performance pay to be distributed among teams rather than to individuals.

Career Planning and Departmental Identity

The Establishment Department had always seen itself as responsible for planning individuals' careers, so that they would be qualified for promotion when then the time came, and to make sure that the Home Office had a sufficient number of suitably qualified staff to fill posts in the future. There was tradition, and an expectation, that staff went where they were told and were promoted when their time came on the basis of their annual reports and an interview with a promotion board. People were now becoming more competitive and career conscious; there was no longer an assumption or even an expectation that anyone would spend a whole career in one department, or even in the Civil Service pressure within the Home Office for more posts to be advertised within the Civil Service, and from the Treasury for them to be advertised publicly. Transfers between departments were becoming more common, often at the instigation of individual managers who wanted to choose 'their own people'. Career and succession planning began to be neglected.[3]

---

3.   The report of a 'Capability Review' carried out in 2006 said 'The culture within the Senior Civil Service also needs to place greater value on the corporate responsibility for talent management, and staff development and redeployment' (Prime Minister's Delivery Unit, *A Capability Review of the Home Office*, London: Cabinet Office, 2006). In a paper written at that time ('Transforming the Home Office'. *Prison Service Journal*, 171, 17-23, 2007). I argued that talent has to be 'grown' as well as 'managed', and so do expertise and the neglected quality of wisdom. The point applied not only in the public sector but also to services commissioned from the private sector, where providers might prefer 'to buy' in talent and expertise from the public sector rather than take responsibility for developing it themselves—see *Appendices 1* and *2*.

Those changes were in many ways necessary and inevitable, but the rapid movement of staff between posts and government departments also brought a loss of departmental identity and continuity, and sometimes of a sense of purpose. Senior officers, including Sir Alexander Maxwell as Permanent Secretary and Sir Lionel Fox as Chairman of the Prison Commission, had given talks on the Department's identity and culture 40 years before, and I had found them a valuable point of reference and sometimes a source of inspiration. In a talk, subsequently produced as an internal paper,[4] I described the history and changing character of the Home Office as follows

'Our history does not, I am afraid, give us a tradition of vision or radical reform. There have been exceptions, for example, in the Prison Service of Ruggles-Brise and later Alexander Paterson, but intellectual and moral leadership in matters of penal and social policy has usually come from outside the Department. In earlier times it came from the great figures of the 18th and 19th-centuries such as Samuel Romilly, John Howard, Elizabeth Fry and Josephine Butler, whose work the interest groups and voluntary organizations try in their own way to carry on today. More recently it has come from the Royal Commissions and other independent inquiries by committees or individuals. The Home Office role is to recognise and seize the opportunities for reform when they present themselves; but at the same time to keep a practical eye on cost and affordability, and on efficient and effective implementation; to avoid the dangers of political over-reaction or short-term opportunism; and to maintain a consistent sense of direction.'

I went on to discuss the nature of civil servants' relationship with ministers—see *Chapter 11*.

Women and Minorities

The Home Office was becoming more acutely aware of discriminatory practices in the way in which women were treated at meetings and the difficulties they could face when one or two women were on their own in an otherwise all-male group. We were only just beginning to use 'he or she' as a matter of course in conversation or written documents. Women were still liable to be treated, for example at meetings with the police, as if they were expected

---

4.   Internal Home Office publication. See also *Chapter 11*.

to make the coffee,[5] although several heads of divisions in key areas of the Department were now women. As well as bringing women's issues to notice and demanding action to resolve them, they adopted a more collaborative and collegiate style of working, in contrast with the more 'territorial' and sometimes competitive attitudes of some of their male colleagues. The criminal justice conferences proved to be a useful vehicle for exposing the subject to discussion. I promoted developments such as flexible working hours and child care, and helped to bring about a situation where the Home Office had the highest proportion of women in the senior open structure of any Whitehall department.

The Home Office did quite well statistically in the number of people in professional or managerial positions who came from ethnic minorities, although most of them were either prison doctors or specialist advisers, and there were not many in the main administrative grades. Increasing but still small numbers were being appointed in the executive and clerical grades, but not yet in the 'fast stream'. We sometimes heard racist remarks at meetings and conferences, but I do not remember anyone making them within the Home Office itself, or any instance where race relations came to notice as a problem in the workplace, although this is not to say that problems did not exist.

Personal Responsibility and the Emerging Culture of Blame

The Home Office was rightly becoming more transparent and accountable (see *Chapter 11*), and more attention was being given to the performance and responsibility of individual members of staff. A less welcome feature was an emerging culture of blame, illustrated by the reaction to the escape of a high security prisoner from Brixton Prison. The escape had been the result of a chapter of minor accidents for which several people were equally responsible and it could have been prevented if any one of them had acted differently at separate points in time. The Home Secretary, then Kenneth Baker, wanted someone to be identified and punished, but for complicated

---

5.   On one occasion a successful entrant to the Civil Service fast stream arrived in the Home Office with a report from the Final Selection Board which referred appreciatively to her dress and appearance and to the engagement ring 'sparkling on her left hand'. The Civil Service Commission were surprised and hurt when we pointed out those comments were not appropriate.

reasons only one of those involved was subject to Home Office discipline. The Home Secretary insisted that he should be made subject to a disciplinary charge, which I had to hear, but what the person had done was more an oversight or an error of judgement than a serious lapse of duty, of a kind which might happen at any time when people are under pressure but rarely with such serious consequences. The others were probably more culpable than he was, and the fault lay more in the structure—the lack of accountability and definition of the roles and responsibilities in the prison and at headquarters—than in neglect on the part of any individual. I dismissed the charge, but the person had been publicly identified and vilified, and kept in a state of uncertainty for several weeks.

The episode also illustrated the complexity which can usually be found when a serious operational failure takes place. It showed that when things go seriously wrong the fault can rarely be attributed to one or two individuals alone, and that the wider context of political and management pressures, local culture and professional ethos has also to be taken into account. There may be no excuse but there will usually be plenty of reasons, and it may be more important to understand the reasons and learn the lessons from them than to punish individuals. The fault may sometimes lie with lax procedures or misguided practices for which senior managers and sometimes ministers are responsible. The dismissal of John Marriott as governor of Parkhurst Prison in 1995 was another, more serious, example.[6]

Prison Service Agency

In 1980 the Cabinet Office's Efficiency Unit published its report on Management in Government.[7] It proposed that large parts of government should become 'executive agencies', their characteristics being a degree of independence from ministers and their departments' central administration in matters of staff and budgetary control, and the separation of 'policy' from 'operations'. It was a major part of government policy at the time, and there was pressure from the Treasury and from ministers to move as much work

---

6.   Governor of Parkhurst prison, effectively dismissed by Michael Howard as Home Secretary in 1995.

7.   Kate Jenkins, Karen Caines and Andrew Jackson, *Improving Efficiency in Government: the Next Steps. Report to the Prime Minister,* London: HMSO, 1988.

to executive agencies as possible. Within the Home Office, it fell to the Establishment Department to formulate the Home Office view on which parts of the office might become 'executive agencies': the Passport Office and the Forensic Science Service were obvious candidates and their eventual transition to agency status created no serious problems. The Prison Service presented more difficulty: it was a much larger undertaking, and a much greater prize from the Treasury's point of view.

The advantages claimed for agency status were that it might give the service a sharper managerial focus, a stronger sense of managerial accountability and a greater feeling of corporate identity, and I thought it would probably do no harm. I was however concerned that the service's culture might become even more inward-looking, with yet less interest in communication with other services or with the Probation Division and other parts of the Home Office.[8] It would not be practicable to separate 'policy' from 'operations' in the Prison Service context, even if the difference could be satisfactorily defined. To do that would have demanded a new administrative structure within the central Home Office to carry the 'policy' responsibilities,[9] and such a division of responsibility would have been an administrative nightmare, resembling the situation which led to the dissolution of the Prison Commission in 1963. It would sometimes be convenient for ministers to use agency status as an excuse for distancing themselves from responsibility for 'operational' failures, although it would often be difficult in practice to distinguish an operational disaster from a defect in policy. In practice, ministers would always find it hard to resist responding to any criticism that 'prisons are too soft', and they ought not as a matter of principle to deny accountability for institutions whose purpose is to deprive people of their liberty and which represent the ultimate power of the state over its citizens. Agency status probably did bring some benefits for the Prison Service but not the transformation or the new constitutional relationship which its proponents sometimes claimed would follow.

---

8.   Those problems would have become even more serious if Prison Service Headquarters had been relocated to Derby, as was being seriously proposed, again with pressure from the Treasury and with support from the Prison Service itself. A lot of effort went into preparing for the move but the proposal was later abandoned on grounds of cost.

9.   A small unit reporting to the Permanent Secretary was created and existed for a time, but it was clear that such a token structure could never work in practice and it was soon disbanded.

Contracting-out and the Private Sector — Prisons

The issues of privatisation, contracting-out, outsourcing and commissioning were more significant. The question whether it can ever be right that an institution which exercises the power of the state to detain people against their will should ever be run for private gain was debated throughout the 1980s. In 1987 Douglas Hurd said in the House of Commons that he did not 'think the House would accept a case for ... handing the business of keeping prisoners safe to anyone other than government servants'.[10] Leon Radzinowicz[11] later argued more vehemently that privatisation

> ...flagrantly violates what I consider to be a fundamental principle. Detention, control and care of prisoners should not be parcelled out to entrepreneurs operating according to market forces, but should remain the undiluted responsibility of the state.

The arguments in favour of contracting-out to the private sector were of three kinds — the effect on relations with the Prison Officers' Association, savings in cost, and the political aim of 'shrinking the state'. For the Home Office and the Prison Service the most immediate and powerful argument was the restraining effect on industrial action by the POA and the strength it would bring to management's bargaining position in the negotiations that were taking place over the long overdue overhaul of prison officers' terms and conditions of service. Another argument, more important in the longer term, was the incentive to improve the management of a prison through the prospect that it might be put out to competitive tender. Contracting-out was assumed to yield savings in cost, mainly in respect of staffing by employing fewer staff at lower rates of pay, but there was no hard evidence about the full costs that might be involved, and none at all on the difference there might be in qualitative terms such as prison discipline, relations between prisoners and staff, rehabilitation and the effect on reoffending.

The third argument was still in the background but was being quietly promoted by 'right-leaning' think tanks and some Conservative Members of Parliament. A green paper published in 1988 canvassed the possibility of

10.   Official Report HC, 16 July 1987, col. 1299.
11.   Radzinowicz, L (1999), *Adventures in Criminology*, London: Routledge, page 432.

contracting-out court and escort duties and involving the private sector in the management of remand prisons,[12] where the objections of principle were somehow thought to be less important than they were for prisoners who had been convicted. In the event, following a visit to the United States by the prisons minister, Lord Caithness and, with little further consultation, ministers decided that the Bill for the Criminal Justice Act 1991 should provide not only for the contracting-out of court and escort duties but also for the management of any existing or future prisons.

I had been attracted ten years earlier by the idea of a borstal run by the charity Community Service Volunteers—see *Chapter 2*—but for the private sector now to be involved presented a different situation. I did not see any serious problem about contracting-out specific functions within prisons, such as catering, education or treatment for drug addiction, provided that the prison itself stayed under public management (although I thought it a pity if it meant that such work would no longer be done by prisoners themselves); but outsourcing a whole prison was another matter. I was most concerned that those competing for contracts would become powerful and politically influential companies which would press for new prisons to be built and more people to be sent to prison in order to increase their profits and benefit their shareholders. I was not yet concerned about the effects of the 'market state' on relationships and values—see *Chapters 11* and *12*—but I was unsure whether the Prison Service would have the skills in commissioning that it would need if it was successfully to negotiate contracts with commercially sophisticated and perhaps unscrupulous providers.

Later evaluations have shown that it is impossible to say that private sector prisons as such are always 'better' or 'worse' than those it the public sector.[13] There are wide variations between prisons in each sector, in the relationships between staff and prisoners, and in the way in which staff use their authority.[14] Different views can be held on whether a commercial contract is

12. Home Office, *Private Sector Involvement in the Remand System* (Cm 434), London: HMSO, 1988.
13. See for example the National Audit Office, *The Operational Performance of PFI Prisons: Report by the Comptroller and Auditor General*, HC700 Session 2002-2003, London: Stationery Office, 2003.
14. Alison Liebling, Ben Crewe and Susan Hulley (2011) 'Values and Practices in Public and Private Sector Prisons: A Summary of Key Findings from an Evaluation', *Prison Service Journal*, no 196, 2011, pages 55-58.

a more effective, or adequate, basis for prison's accountability as compared with a public prison's accountability to ministers and Parliament. My fear that politically powerful contractors would argue for the greater use of prison sentences did not materialise, but the more subtle consequences of largescale involvement by international corporations, the influences they can bring to bear, their long-term effect on relationships and dynamics, and the costs of operational or financial failure, are still uncertain. A prison governor who left the public Prison Service for the private sector has commented[15]

> … it is a commercial organization, so there's a bottom line which is financial. I've reached the tentative conclusion that this is no worse, and in some ways more honest, than the equivalent bottom line in the public sector, which was fundamentally political. Both are frustrating when the bottom line for the best individuals actually working in the system is simply to do good for those most affected by it.

I return to the wider question of the relationship between public services, the private sector and the state in *Chapter 11*.

The Home Office as I Left It

We did not often stop to ask 'How are we doing?' as a question about the Home Office as a department of state (Brian Cubbon's seminars in 1982 were an exception). The Home Office had become less tolerant of eccentricity and poor performance than it had been 30 years before, and there was more emphasis on financial discipline, management, performance and appraisal. It was more politically and publicly accountable, with a greater awareness of, and attention to, the political context and ministers who were more closely involved. The mechanisms of audit and inspection became more numerous and effective with the creation of the Audit Commission and the creation or strengthening of the inspectorates of prisons, probation and magistrates' courts.

Within the Home Office, office services had greatly improved. The photocopier and later the fax machine had transformed the way in which papers were handled and the 'file' was losing its significance, although it is hard to tell what effect, if any, there might have been on the speed or quality of

---

15. Personal correspondence.

decision-making. Email and desktop computers were still in the future. The old structure of departments and divisions was still more or less in place but the Home Office had grown greatly in size. The Immigration Department was now in Croydon and the Prison Department in Cleland House, but most of the rest of the Department was at Queen Anne's Gate, in the building now refurbished and occupied by the Ministry of Justice. The old Whitehall building was becoming a distant memory.

The Home Office had probably become more accessible, accountable and responsive, and we had probably helped the criminal justice services to do the same. The temporary relief provided by the fall in the prison population after 1988 helped the Prison Service through a period when its situation was especially precarious. Prisons were now more safe and secure and prisoners were treated more fairly and with more dignity, although physical conditions were still too often deplorable and women and young offenders had come to be seriously neglected. The Probation Service had improved its management and its credibility to a point where it was able to survive the attacks which followed, although at the price that has been described in *Chapter 7*. The Police and Criminal Evidence Act 1984 and the formation of the Crown Prosecution Service had brought greater integrity to the process of law enforcement. Minorities and victims of crime came to be treated with more consideration and respect and their voices were more often heard, but serious issues remained. From the Criminal Statistics and the then British Crime Survey, and from research and opinion surveys, the Home Office had become better informed about the nature and extent of crime, its impact and consequences, and of the means by which it might be prevented and reduced. We were more ready to look for and find ways in which crime might be reduced, and to encourage or introduce them where we could.

Most of those are matters of impression and judgement. We did not yet have any quantified measurements apart from the regular statistics and evaluations of particular projects, and no clear idea what such measurements might be. We did not think that criminal justice could be judged only in terms of its supposed effects on crime, either in practice (how could its effect be separated from those of other influences that were at work?), or as a matter of principle. That was not what criminal justice was for.[16] We did however ask ourselves 'How are we doing?' in our own areas of work. That was relatively straightforward in the job I was doing in the Prison Department in the early 1970s despite some regrets, for example over the rebuilding of Holloway as I have explained in *Chapter 2*. I thought I had been reasonably successful in my later posting to the Prison Department, and that I had made some contribution to giving the Prison Service a stronger sense of direction and purpose, and to civilising prisons themselves, but I was still acutely conscious that much more needed to be done, and that what we did at that time had made only a small impact on the problems of the Prison Service and of imprisonment in England and Wales more generally.

The question was even more difficult in relation to the wider responsibilities for criminal justice which I assumed in 1982. There were some mistakes and some disappointments, especially over the Criminal Justice Act 1991 and I thought over drugs, as I described in *Chapters 8 and 9*. We established a more coordinated approach among the three government departments concerned with criminal justice in Whitehall —the Home Office, the then Lord Chancellor's Department and the Law Officers' Department including (later) the Crown Prosecution Service—and between the criminal justice services themselves, although not at that stage across Whitehall or local services more generally. We did, I think, succeed in formulating and starting to put into effect a coherent strategy for crime and criminal justice, including legislation but also—and I believe in the long-term more important—crime prevention, the treatment of minorities and support for victims. I could not claim to have done much to reduce crime, but I hope that some of what we did may have contributed to the reduction which began in the mid-1990s.

The Home Office was less sure of itself, but also less complacent, about what it was doing than it had been at the end of the 1950s. That was partly a reaction to years of public criticism which had become stronger and more pervasive than it had been 30 years previously, but more was being expected and we wanted to do more ourselves—to reduce crime, to raise standards for the treatment and rehabilitation of offenders, and to improve the quality of justice. We thought we were doing the best we could and I believe we

---

16. Although I occasionally and thoughtlessly spoke as if it might be. I was once politely but firmly corrected when I spoke on those lines to a meeting of magistrates in Manchester.

made progress in all those respects, but across all the Department's main functions — policing, immigration, prisons and crime — we seemed by the 1990s always to be managing or avoiding crises of various kinds and it was hard to look beyond those to a vision of a better future or to know how to achieve it if we could. The Home Office, and government as a whole, was in today's language linear, analogue and top-down, while the world around us was becoming increasingly complex, horizontal and plural. Without appreciating the full significance of the changes that were taking place, and without conceptualising the situation in those terms, I tried to respond to them through the understandings and relationships that I tried to encourage and develop.

I always found value in bringing people from different positions and backgrounds together to share experiences and ideas, and doing so in settings where they could feel comfortable and confident. I thought it important to get out of the office, to see what happens on the ground and meet people in their own working situations. As civil servants we needed to listen, respond and explain, and not just to say and tell. I did not expect to have original or inspirational ideas of my own, but I did try to encourage situations and relationships from which ideas could emerge, to make connections and encourage lateral thinking, and then to take ideas forward through the administrative process. I tried to show appreciation and give credit when it was due, although I may not have done that as often as I should.

I find it sad that the Home Office should so many times have been perceived as a 'failing' department, and criminal justice as a 'failing' service or institution. There have some operational and administrative disasters and there has always been room for improvement, but criticism has sometimes been the consequence of unrealistic expectations, failures of understanding or attempts to score political points for which both ministers and civil servants bear some responsibility. It may be that Home Office 'mandarins' or policy-makers were a (mostly) Oxbridge elite who had little experience of life as it was lived by large sections of the population, but I do not think we were as complacent, self-seeking or obstructive as some critics have described us as being. The caricatures and relationships portrayed in the television comedy *Yes, Minister* were plausible enough to provide good entertainment, but they had little resemblance to any situations I had experienced in real life. For all its entertainment value, I believe the series and the way it was interpreted did serious damage to ministers and civil servants alike.

The Home Office, with the Ministry of Justice as it now is, is a department to which I am still proud to have given most of my working life.

CHAPTER 11

Principles, Values and Culture

This chapter collects together a number of impressions and thoughts on some more general subjects which reveal the character of the Home Office, what it was like to work there, what we were trying to do and what we believed in. We always tried to do 'the right thing', and for the most part that was a matter of doing what had to be done — responding to events, managing a crisis, handling the business, interpreting and applying policy, administering the process. Judgements were more often about how to do things than about whether they were the right things to do. If they were the wrong things, we would usually expect that to be a matter for ministers, perhaps as a result of a public campaign with which we might or might not privately sympathise.

We did however feel a sense of 'the rightness of things', both as civil servants but also, and sometimes perhaps especially, as members of the Home Office where we were in a sense the guardians of the relationship between the Crown and its subjects (the historical function of the Secretary of State) or in more modern terms between the state and the citizen. The nature of that guardianship[1] was never made explicit, but it was part of the 'living tradition' of which Sir Charles Cunningham spoke in his talk in 1959 — see *Chapter 1*.

Ministers and Officials

Ministers became more active during the 1970s and especially the 1980s. The change had begun in the Home Office when Roy Jenkins became Home Secretary in 1965, and it accelerated after Margaret Thatcher became Prime Minister in 1979. More issues engaged their attention and they were keener to take new initiatives and obtain publicity for them. I inevitably became more involved with ministers as I reached more senior positions, and more restricted by political priorities and necessities than I had been in the Prison

---

1. Its decline is the subject of Ian Loader's article 'Fall of the Platonic Guardians: Liberalism, Criminology and Political Responses to Crime in England and Wales', *British Journal of Criminology* (2006), 46, 561-586.

Department in the early 1970s. The understanding was that ministers would set the political framework and give a sense of direction, but they would for the most part expect officials to propose particular actions or policies. I became used to situations where I had to do things I would prefer not to do or where things I would like to do were unaffordable, impracticable or politically unrealistic, but there was always some space for officials to take initiatives of our own and act on them, so long as we were confident that ministers agreed and would support us if necessary.

It was clear that as civil servants and 'servants of the Crown' our first loyalty was to our ministers and our duty was to do what they expected. We had to accept that policies and schemes to which we had committed ourselves might be abandoned, to learn to live with disappointment, and to be resilient and resourceful in responding to new demands and situations. It was our job to help and enable ministers to do what they wanted; civil servants should not have personal agendas; and they must certainly not try to obstruct anything that ministers have decided or prejudice what they were likely to decide. The civil servant should be able and expected to form his or her own independent judgement. It might sometimes be necessary to give a minister unwelcome advice — for example that a scheme is not well thought out, will have unintended consequences or will be vulnerable to legal challenge. He or she should not be afraid to do that if necessary, but should always try to have options or solutions to offer and not just to point out difficulties. It would be an abdication of responsibility to comply unthinkingly with what seems to be expected, for example with the excuse that 'it's my job', without regard for its implications or consequences, or for its legitimacy or propriety. For my generation, the memory of the Second World War was too recent for 'I was only doing what I was told' to be an acceptable excuse.

Christopher Hood and Martin Lodge[2] have described the relationship between ministers and public servants in terms of a 'bargain'. It may be broadly of two kinds, although neither excludes the other. Public servants may be treated as trustees, constituting a self-managed autonomous estate; or as agents who are servants of their political masters. The former view, if it is still held at all in this country, would now been seen as elitist, old-fashioned

2.   Christopher Hood and Martin Lodge, *The Politics of Public Service Bargains: Reward, Competency, Loyalty — and Blame,* Oxford University Press, 2006.

and a relic of an earlier age; the latter would seem more modern and democratic, and successive governments' reforms have moved the Civil Service further in that direction. I could never subscribe to the former view without qualification, but something may be lost if it is abandoned altogether.

The question whether civil servants have any identity separate from the minister was mentioned in *Chapter 1* and in Hugo Young's bicentenary lecture—see *Chapter 5*. How far the Civil Service is or should be independent of the government of the day, and whether civil servants have any duties or loyalties apart from those owed to their minister, became an issue during the 1980s. The Secretary of the Cabinet, Sir Robert (now Lord) Armstrong, sought to resolve the question in his *Note by the Head of the Home Civil Service on the Duties and Responsibilities of Civil Servants in Relation to Ministers,* known as the 'Armstrong Memorandum',[3] where he said that 'civil servants are the servants of the Crown. For all practicable purposes the Crown in this context is represented by the government of the day.' The memorandum was generally welcomed in the Civil Service, and it became heresy to express any disagreement with it.

I thought the situation was rather more complex. Although our duties to the Crown were normally indistinguishable from those we owed to ministers, our duties of integrity, impartiality, care, thoughtfulness, thorough preparation and attention to detail—now set out in the Civil Service Code—were not entirely at ministers' disposal and should not be compromised for the sake of good relations with ministers or the advancement of one's career. Ministers themselves have a duty to the Crown to place the public or national interest above those of their political party or their own political careers—in the words of the Privy Council oath, to 'in all things … do as a faithful and true Servant ought to do to Her Majesty'; and both ministers and civil servants have a duty to observe the Rule of Law. If a disagreement takes place, it should be openly discussed and differences should be respected, on the understanding that the minister has the final decision having considered

---

3.   Robert Armstrong, *The Duties and Responsibilities of Civil Servants in Relation to Ministers,*
      Note by the Head of the Home Civil Service, London: Cabinet Office, 1985, amended version
      1994.

advice and taken those differences unto account.[4]

In the paper *Continuity and Change* which I wrote shortly before leaving the Home Office, I said

> ... the official's relationship with Ministers is emphatically not one of passive obedience. It is not the official's job to give Ministers the advice they want to hear, but to make sure that the financial, practical and other consequences of a course of action have been properly worked out, and are firmly in the Minister's minds, before a decision is taken. It is a serious professional failure on our part if we are unprepared, or so anxious to please that we fail to provide properly thought out judgement or advice. The other side of the relationship is that Ministers should respect and expect that advice, even if they decide not to accept it. If that happens, it is the duty of officials to give effect to the decision unless they can be moved to other work, or in an extreme case they are prepared to resign.

The two sides of the formal relationship between officials and Ministers are set out in Sir Robert (now Lord) Armstrong's memorandum of 1 December 1987. While emphasising the civil servant's duty to serve their Ministers with integrity and to the best of their ability, that memorandum concentrates on the passive and negative aspects of our job—to do as we are told, to do it discreetly if not in secret, and avoid acting independently. Most of us joined the civil service in the expectation that we would have the opportunity to serve the public in a more positive way by developing our own ideas (or just picking up the ideas of others); by arranging them in a coherent order; by carrying them into the decision-making process; and eventually if we persuade Ministers that they are good ideas, by putting them into effect. This is what most of us still hope to do, and what I believe we ought to do.

It is our job to see that Ministers have a choice of realistic and properly thought out options available to them, especially at the stage when a new policy is to be introduced. To do that we need to use our judgement and imagination, to create

---

4. The Ministerial Code now states that 'Ministers must uphold the political impartiality of the Civil Service and not ask civil servants to act in anyway which would conflict with the *Civil Service Code* as set out in the *Constitutional Reform and Governance Act 2010*...Ministers have a duty to give fair consideration and due weight to informed and impartial advice from civil servants, as well as to other considerations and advice in reaching policy decisions ...'.

situations in which new ideas can emerge, to test those ideas in discussion with colleagues and professional contacts, and to subject them to research and statistical analysis, often at a stage well before the issue reaches the point of Ministerial decision or engages Ministers' serious attention. It is hard work—it needs space and skill, and it needs persistence and commitment. It involves a considerable degree of openness with those inside and outside the Office, and therefore a certain amount of risk and courage to face it. It is not easy to reconcile with the unrelenting pressure under which most of us have to work, and although procedures like the annual performance review and the strategic planning exercise can and should support it, we have always to make sure that those procedures do not become formalised, inward looking and bureaucratic.

Hugo Young had asked in his bicentenary lecture in 1982 whether the Home Office existed only through the person of the Home Secretary, as the conventional doctrine supposed, or whether it could have an identity and culture of its own, as he implied it should. I always believed that the Home Office had an identity, traditions, a collective memory and a commitment to humanity and 'freedom under the law' which survived changes of Home Secretary. They gave a sense of continuity and pride in the Department, and most Home Secretaries also respected and valued them, as I think Whitelaw and Callaghan had acknowledged in the bicentenary lectures—see *Chapters 1* and *5*. I do not know if that survives; if not something valuable has been lost.

Procedural Justice

By the 1970s, government's lack of transparency and its shortcomings in responding to the expectations of its users and the wider public were becoming apparent and other mechanisms came to be added. In criminal justice, I described in *Chapter 3* I how we tried to make boards of visitors more effective in their oversight of prison practices and conditions, and in *Chapter 4* the formation of the new Inspectorate of Prisons. A more independent Inspectorate of Probation and a Prisons Ombudsman (later the Prisons and Probation Ombudsman) followed. Prisoners became increasingly ready and able to challenge the department in the domestic courts, and sometimes at the European Court of Human Rights.

Decisions by the courts sometimes helped or compelled the service to introduce reforms, such as relaxations over prisoners' correspondence and censorship, which I personally welcomed although the Prison Department had resisted them at the time. They had the advantage that prison officers were more ready to accept changes that were legal requirements than they would have been if they had been management decisions. The judgements of the European Court of Human Rights on release from life sentences, especially those in the cases of Thynne, Wilson and Gunnell, and the principle that release should be decided by a judicial or 'court-like' authority and not by ministers or officials, were also important and have been described in Lord Windlesham's *Responses to Crime.*[5] Lord Wilberforce's judgement in *Raymond v. Honey*[6] stated that 'Under English law a convicted prisoner, in spite of his imprisonment, retains all the civil rights which are not taken away expressly or by necessary implication', although its effects were in the event very limited.

A significant development during the 1980s was the expansion of judicial review, across government as a whole. Some civil servants, and ministers, saw (and still see) the process as unnecessarily intrusive and sometimes as damaging interference in the proper conduct of public business. I welcomed such interventions, both for increasing the Department's accountability to the public and as a valuable discipline to improve the quality of the decision-making process, and did my best to encourage a positive attitude towards rulings of the courts. I arranged a seminar where one of the Department's legal advisers explained how the process operated and might affect the work they were doing. I encouraged colleagues not to see it as a threat or to try and circumvent it by going out of their way to make decisions 'judge proof', but as providing a valuable discipline to improve the quality of the decision-making process. The government later published *The Judge Over Your Shoulder*, now in its fourth edition, more defensive but with a similar line of argument.

In a lecture to JUSTICE in 1990 I felt able to say, perhaps rather complacently, that

---

5.   13 ECHR 135. See also Lord Windlesham, *Responses to Crime, Penal Policy in the Making*, Vol 2, Oxford: Clarendon Press, 1993, pages 347 *et seq.*

6.   *Raymond v. Honey* [1982] 1 All ER 756,759.

The Home Office has a traditional concern for keeping the proper balance between freedom and respect for the individual on the one hand and the protection of society on the other, sometimes expressed as 'freedom under the law'. That concern is especially acute in areas such as terrorism, immigration and asylum, and miscarriages of justice, but it may not always have been apparent and the Department has on occasions given an impression of secrecy or arrogance which has produced suspicion and distrust. Important changes are nevertheless taking place in the way in which the Office conducts its business. In many respects there is now more openness; greater readiness to consult and to listen as well as explain; and a recognition that policies cannot work successfully if they are simply imposed on operational services, the judiciary and others by legislation or government circular without preparation and consultation.

Those concerned with giving effect to those policies have to feel their own sense of ownership and that policies belong to themselves as well as to the government of the day. They must be committed to their success for their own sake and on their own merits, not just because they are what the central administration expects. Procedural justice and the ability to be heard are increasingly important aspects of Home Office administration, including the administration of prisons and the parole system, and all matters affecting ethnic minorities. The active interest of bodies such as JUSTICE and Amnesty International is valuable and often effective. In this context, the country's obligations under international human rights instruments are a necessary reminder of the standards which we should set for ourselves and which others are entitled to expect from us; the dangers of lack of attention and of ill-judged concessions to short-term pressures would be much greater without them. They can be a useful support or point of reference for changes which are separately justified on their own merits. They can help to reinforce the political will, professional leadership, collective integrity and individual conscience on which fairness and justice ultimately depend.

Human Rights

Statutory protection of human rights was not a matter of serious concern to the Home Office during the 1980s. We had been brought up in a tradition which assumed that the democratic process combined with the integrity of the country's public servants and elected representatives could be relied upon to prevent injustice or correct it if it occurred. Like most of my Home Office colleagues, I believed that natural justice, fairness and freedom under the law were best protected by a democratically elected government working through government departments and statutory services in which the best traditions and highest standards of public service were rigorously maintained. I had an instinctive preference for administrative decision-making (by ministers or people like ourselves), rather than legal proceedings and judicial adjudication. We assumed that the rights guaranteed by the United Nations Universal Declaration of Human Rights and the European Convention on Human Rights were fully protected by our unwritten constitutional arrangements and common law, and we expected the European Court of Human Rights to be fairly static in its interpretation and application of the European Convention.

The judgements of the Court were however beginning to have a considerable and sometimes unexpected impact on United Kingdom law and practice. The Home Office contested them at the time, but my own view was that their impact was generally helpful rather than otherwise, and that it had given greater impetus for changes that were controversial but sooner or later had to be made. Examples included prisoners' correspondence, the interception of telephone calls, and corporal punishment in schools. The need to ask 'What about Strasbourg?' as well as 'What about judicial review?' was also a healthy discipline in the formulation of policy and the drafting of legislation more generally.

I came face to face with the issues when I had to prepare and then present the United Kingdom's five-yearly report on its compliance with the United Nations Universal Declaration of Human Rights to the UN Human Rights Committee in 1985. Rather to the surprise of the voluntary organizations, I invited them to a meeting to discuss what we should say in the report and how it might deal with some of the sensitive issues such as Northern Ireland. In the report and at the meeting in New York where I was accompanied by the Home Office legal adviser, Anthony Hammond, I tried not to be defensive, to admit that there were areas for concern, and to show that the UK took those concerns seriously even when no immediate solution seemed to be in prospect. I was asked questions about subjects which included the position of the Falkland Islands and the British Indian Ocean Territories, safeguards for racial and sexual equality, immigration, detention without trial, the use of arms by the security services, the treatment of prisoners and mental health patients, privacy and family life, and freedom of thought and expression.

The most difficult questions, and those with which the committee was most concerned, were those relating to Northern Ireland and human rights, and specifically about how the United Kingdom could claim to be protecting fundamental human rights and freedoms in accordance with the declaration when they were not protected by Act of Parliament, for example by incorporating the European Convention into domestic legislation. I gave the conventional answer that all those rights exist or subsist in the system of common law unless they are expressly removed by statute, and that an individual who believes their rights to have been infringed could be protected by Parliament, judicial review, and in the end by recourse to the European Court. I said there was not sufficient support for new legislation in Parliament at present, the argument being that new legislation would add little or nothing to the protection that was already provided and would run the risk of damaging conflict between the judiciary and the executive.[7]

After I left the Home Office, in a paper written for Charter 88 in 1994, I repeated those arguments but said that the situation and my own views had changed. I referred to the concern among public servants about what they saw as the break up of the state and the sacrifice of the public interest to theories of competition and market forces; and to a wider social concern about the divisions that were appearing in British, but perhaps especially English, society and the instability, alienation and sense of injustice that were associated with them. I argued that there was now a more urgent case for a framework of administrative and constitutional law within which it would be possible to submit proposals or decisions to tests of constitutionality or the public interest, separate from the political interests of the party in office.

7.　The record concluded that 'Members of the Committee thanked the United Kingdom delegation for its co-operation and for its detailed answers, which had provided valuable information demonstrating the achievements of the United Kingdom in implementing the Covenant...It was, however, felt that there were still gaps in the implementation of certain articles of the Covenant and with regard to a comprehensive system of remedies......The Chairman...welcomed the very satisfactory manner in which the dialogue with the United Kingdom had continued and warmly thanked the delegation for its constructive role in that dialogue and its efforts to provide detailed replies.' United Nations *Report of the Human Rights Committee*, General Assembly's Official Records, Fortieth Session, Supplement No 40 (A/40/40), New York: United Nations, 1985.

Within or alongside that framework there would be some formal recognition of civil and political rights, most obviously through the incorporation of the European Convention into domestic law, although that would be one possibility among others.

Even so, I was still sceptical about new legislation, pointing out that there was still a strong tradition of English pragmatism which preferred to think of citizenship more in terms of responsibilities, obligations and expectations than of formal rights protected by law, and expressed doubts about the interactions between Parliament, the executive and the courts that would follow. I further argued that a Bill of Rights would not by itself guarantee the fairness and impartiality of government, or its disinterested commitment to the national interest. Those would still depend on the integrity, vision and commitment of ministers and officials, and on the attitudes and values of society as a whole. A higher priority as I then saw it was for reforms such as a new approach to public accountability, especially in the context of privatisation and contracting-out; changes in the procedure for making public and especially judicial appointments; a new emphasis on information, analysis and research; improvements in Parliamentary procedure; and new legislation such as a Freedom of Information Act or a Civil Service Act. Wider problems in society might be addressed through a revitalisation of local government, the overhaul and better coordination of various social policies, and possibly electoral reform.

That was 20 years ago. Those concerns remain, but I have been persuaded by the view that the country needed to 'bring rights home', and to be able to deal with complaints of abuse of human rights in its domestic courts without the delay and expense of recourse to Strasbourg. The Human Rights Act as it was enacted in 1998 was probably the best available means of achieving that objective. I now believe that governments could not be relied upon to secure human rights without a strong, independent and if necessary assertive judiciary; that citizens' rights and freedom are better protected by the courts than they are likely to be by government; and that governments must themselves be subject to the Rule of Law.

My regret is that a culture is now developing which is one of technical compliance and of finding means to circumvent the law, and not one of personal integrity and principled judgement; and that the Human Rights

Act has come to be seen as an obstacle to be overcome, not a standard to live up to.

Public Services and the State

The Conservative government in the 1980s paid greater attention than previous administrations to the accountability of public services, including especially those that were not part of the Civil Service. The main focus was at first on financial management, on efficiency and effectiveness, and on the mechanisms of targets and indicators and inspection and audit in order to improve performance. Services' accountability was seen as being primarily through their own management structures and then to government and Parliament. That was the context of most of our work with the criminal justice services at that time, and I had no difficulty with it. But the government also began to promote more direct forms of accountability to the public, now seen as the 'consumer' or 'customer' and with an emphasis on 'choice' and the 'market' as part of this model. One example was the 'Citizen's Charter', with its the 'Charter Mark' for services that met the required standard. Significantly, it was a charter for individuals to exert pressure as consumers, not for the public or for citizens as a whole. 'Choice' was between those things that were on offer: 'customers' were not able to say they wanted something else instead. The charter was presented as a effective way of 'driving up standards' but its origin was in the government's ideological belief in the 'market', with competition between providers and ultimately privatisation.

It soon became obvious, though it was never admitted, that the 'market' would not work for criminal justice. No one could say who the 'consumers' were supposed to be except that they did not include those who were most affected by the service that was provided — defendants, offenders and victims of crime. Providers' commercial freedom would inevitably be constrained by the law and the decisions of the courts. As policies developed, the language of providers and consumers changed to one of commissioners and providers, with government in effect acting as both commissioner and consumer, and the public having no greater choice or influence than they had before. Risk and responsibility would be transferred to the provider, but government would determine the nature and quality of the service to be provided through the terms of its contracts. Providers can be held to account for their performance under the contract, but the transparency needed for democratic accountability is hard to reconcile with commercial confidentiality. If there is a delivery chain which involves several providers, accountability becomes even more diffused and obscure. As Dr Richard Beeching said in the 1960s, commercial enterprise is hard to reconcile with public service.

I have always thought of public service as a personal and professional commitment to the public interest which is more important than a person's own career or the interests of one's employer. It is more a vocation than a particular job or career, and it is not the same as working in the public sector.[8] Its values are not exclusive to the public sector and one sector is not 'better' than the other. But there are very real differences in the structure of their accountability, in their culture, and in what they can properly be expected to do in a democratic society.

A providing body's individual ethos and the way it treats its staff will affect the staff members' relationships with those with whom they work, and ultimately the quality and legitimacy of the service that organization provides. Public service values are harder for an employer to establish and maintain if the aim is to employ staff as cheaply as possible in order to compete for contracts and profits. Competition and especially payment by results are an open invitation to 'gaming', and could encourage providers to neglect those who are less profitable—the vulnerable, disabled or disadvantaged, or socially or economically excluded.

Where the provider is a commercial company, its accountability is not primarily to the government or the public but to its shareholders. Its instinct will always be to expand its market and its profits. In criminal justice the national interest is, or should be, to achieve just and fair outcomes, not to expand the market for those dealing in punishment. There could be a particular tension if the providing organizations are international corporations with no particular British identity or loyalty to the country except for

8.   The former Archbishop of Canterbury Dr Rowan Williams has written of the need to restore 'a vision of public service as a fulfilling and coherent calling, recognised as such in society at large'. Rowan Williams 'Sovereignty, Democracy, Justice: Elements of a Good Society', Eighth lecture in the Magna Carta Lecture Series, hosted by Royal Holloway, University of London and run in association with the Magna Carta Trust. *Justice Reflections*, Issue 35, No. 237, 2014, 11.

the profits they can take from it. Providers working on a large scale might become so powerful and so entrenched that government was unable financially, politically or operationally to terminate their contracts and return the service to the public sector.

Many of the functions performed in criminal justice involve judgements about a person's character and behaviour which may affect that person's liberty and position in society, the situation of their family, and the public's safety. Those are not managerial or commercial judgements and they should be made within a democratically accountable framework, in accordance with due process and professional standards and by public servants who are accountable both to the law and to ministers and ultimately to Parliament, free from considerations of their employers' profitability or commercial advantage. Rules of public accountability should not be replaced by the law of private contract. Where services are commissioned from the private sector, the government should insist on professional standards and the mechanisms needed to sustain them. Training, standards and professional qualifications should be set nationally and periodically reviewed, and performance should be inspected for compliance with those standards as well as the performance of the contract.

Seventy per cent of the work of the Probation Service was at the time of writing being transferred to private sector contractors as part of the Coalition government's programme of 'transforming rehabilitation'. Its details are outside the scope of this volume, but it is a hazardous and ethically questionable enterprise.

CHAPTER 12

Later Years: Social and Political Change, and Some Conclusions

---

This chapter describes what I have done during the 22 years since I left the Home Office, it reflects on the situation as it now appears in the spring of 2014; and it offers some conclusions.

Transition to Oxford

With the support of Roger Hood[1] and Mark Freeland[2] I was able to make my base in Oxford, with positions as an associate at the University of Oxford Centre for Criminological Research, now the Centre for Criminology, and as a supernumerary fellow of St John's College until 1999. I was able to observe the continuing developments from a different and more independent perspective, with the advantage of access to the growing volume of academic literature and an opportunity to contribute to it when I could. My main areas of interest were criminal justice, government, public services and the connections between them, with common themes of citizenship, account-ability, legitimacy and responsibility.

I was pleased to be accepted by the academic community of criminal justice and legal scholars, in Oxford and beyond, and to become more familiar with their perspectives and insights. They included Andrew Ashworth, Ros Burnett, Elizabeth Fisher, Mark Freedland, Roger Hood, Carolyn Hoyle, Nicola Lacey, Ian Loader, Julian Roberts and Lucia Zedner in Oxford; Anthony Bottoms and Alison Liebling in Cambridge; David Downes, Tim Newburn, Robert Reiner and Paul Rock at the London School of Economics; and Mike Hough at King's College, London. Some of them had been members of the discussion group which I mentioned in *Chapter 5*, and Tim Newburn and Mike Hough had been colleagues in the Home Office

---

1. Director of the University of Oxford Centre for Criminological Research and now Professor of Criminology.
2. Fellow of St John's College and now Professor of Employment Law.

Research Unit. They and many others provided stimulation and inspiration, and I have greatly valued their friendship, encouragement and support.

For some years I taught groups of students who were reading Criminal Justice and Penology as part of their undergraduate degree in law. Those traditional Oxford tutorials were some of my most personally rewarding experiences, and I have always been grateful to the students for the enthusiasm they showed for the subject and for the challenges and stimulation they provided.

St John's Seminars

I wanted to use the opportunity to think more coherently about some of the wider issues and underlying principles which had been implied in the work of the Home Office, and now also the Ministry of Justice, as I had understood it—the nature of citizenship and the state and the relationship between them, the rights and responsibilities that they imply, the nature and limits of freedom and human rights, the Rule of Law, and what is meant by the public interest and public duty. Some of my conclusions were set out in the previous chapter.

From 1992 until 1997 Mark Freedland and I arranged a series of seminars at St John's which reviewed the developments that were taking place in public law, citizenship and public administration. The seminars continued the spirit of the conferences I had instituted while I was at the Home Office, with participants from universities, the Civil Service and other public services, but with a wider focus than criminal justice. Each year there was a programme of five or six seminars which discussed a range of subjects relating to issues which were current at the time. They included law reform, accountability, localisation, the emerging 'new public management', market testing, the Citizen's Charter, the Private Finance Initiative, the use of information and research, the legislative process, the case for a Public Service Act, 'social markets', and the role of charities and voluntary organizations. Speakers approached them from different academic perspectives such as law, history, economics, criminology, management, accountancy and public administration; and from different professional backgrounds such as education, policing, the judiciary, the National Health Service and various government departments. Records were prepared and circulated after each programme.

We had no quantified objectives: we were more concerned to expose and examine different considerations and points of view than to reach conclusions or advance particular arguments, but I believe most of those who took part found it a stimulating and enjoyable experience.

After the Labour government took office in 1997, it became evident that the new government did not like its civil servants to associate too freely with academics (they were 'too busy'), and that civil servants would no longer be able to come to seminars of that kind.

Publications and Lectures

Drawing on the seminars at St John's, discussion with colleagues and the rapidly increasing volume of academic literature, I wrote several short articles in journals and newsletters and gave a number of lectures to academic and professional audiences. With the approach of the 1997 election and the prospect of a change of government, I wrote for the Howard League a pamphlet, *Darkness and Light* which suggested the kind of programme which I hoped the new government might adopt. I argued that fear of crime and lack of confidence in the system had led to unrealistic expectations and over-simplification of the issues, and to a concentration on law enforcement and punishment which might be a plausible response to public feeling but not an effective means of reducing crime or dealing with its effects. I drew attention to the increasing prevalence of an 'exclusive' attitude to human behaviour and to society based on social division, personal protection, suspicion and fear; and argued for a more 'inclusive' view which would value and respect diversity, human dignity, compassion and the will to change. I repeated the argument that feasible changes in law enforcement, sentencing or the treatment of offenders were unlikely by themselves to have more than a marginal effect on the general level of crime.

Further articles on subjects such as the role of the National Offender Management Service in civil renewal;[3] public service and leadership in the 21st-century; the prospects for progress in penal reform, with particular reference to the confusion over the nature, purpose and legitimacy of punishment

---

3.   A concept which David Blunkett as Home Secretary developed in his paper *Civil Renewal: A New Agenda,* London: Home Office, 2003. It resembled in some ways the 'big society' promoted by David Cameron during the early days of the Coalition government.

and the government's unrealistic expectations; the rights and especially the responsibilities of prisoners as citizens; and the contribution which prisons as a public service might make to their local communities and the support they might receive from them.[4] Others were about relationships, accountability and responsibility in the National Offender Management Service; civil society, the state and criminal justice and the role of charities; government and public services in Britain when the 'new public management' began to fall from favour; and criminal justice and government at a time of austerity.

Partly at the prompting of my students, I began to assemble the material for *Crime, State and Citizen,* first published in 2001 with a second edition in 2006, and in 2010 Ros Burnett joined me in writing *Where Next for Criminal Justice?*, published in the following year and intended, like *Darkness and Light,* to coincide with a change of government and the possibility of a positive change of direction. I was pleased when the Magistrates' Association asked me soon afterwards to edit a collection of papers[5] on the future of the lay magistracy, in the context of the ever-increasing demands for economy and administrative efficiency, conflicting pressures for greater centralisation or devolution, and the gradual extension of measures to deal with offending which avoid the cost, delay and sometimes uncertainty of prosecution and proceedings in court.

Voluntary Organizations

For several years after the Second World War, governments and statutory services saw the voluntary sector as unimportant. People's needs were to be met not by charity but as an entitlement to be provided by the state. Volunteers got in the way of professionally qualified staff and were more trouble than they were worth. The situation began to change during the 1970s and 1980s as new charities were formed such as Nacro, Victim Support and the Prison Reform Trust in the criminal justice sector, and became important both for the work they did and for their influence on policy and practice and in the country at large. In criminal justice they helped to balance the punitive attitudes which later gathered force in the political parties and some

---

4.   Drawing on some of the ideas which had informed our vision for borstals and the new Holloway 30 years before (see *Chapter 3*), but I hoped in a more practical form.

5.   *The Magistracy at the Crossroads,* Sherfield-on-Loddon: Waterside Press, 2012.

of the newspapers. Governments and commentators increasingly recognised the significance and potential strength of civil society and social capital.

Voluntary organizations working with government and perhaps especially in the criminal justice sector have to manage a constant tension between preserving the independence which is essential for their credibility, integrity and charitable status, and collaborating with — and sometimes accepting funding from — governments whose policies and politics they may not support. Governments, and now private sector companies competing for business, may try to exploit their capacity and goodwill in support of their own political or commercial objectives. Both recognise the voluntary sector's importance and potential for the 'rehabilitation revolution' that is part of the Coalition government's criminal justice policy; the sector should not be excluded but it must be given adequate support and its integrity should not be compromised.

I worked with a number of voluntary and other organizations, often as a trustee or member of council. They included at various times the Magistrates' Association, the Mental Health Foundation, Divert, JUSTICE, the Howard League (of which I was chair for a time), the Runnymede Trust, the Foundation for Outdoor Adventure, the Relationships Foundation, the Criminal Justice Alliance, a National Health Service Trust and, most continuously, the Thames Valley Partnership and the Gilbert Murray Trust. I was chair of Victim Support's working party on compensation for victims of crime; a member of the Prison Reform Trust's commissions on the mandatory life sentence for murder, chaired by the retired Lord Chief Justice Lord Lane, and on women in prison chaired by Dorothy Wedderburn; and a member of the Runnymede Trust's Commission on the Future of Multi-Ethnic Britain chaired by Bhikhu (now Lord) Parekh — see *Chapter 8*. I also gave evidence on several occasions to the Home Affairs and Public Administration Committees of the House of Commons.

The Thames Valley Partnership has always been a special interest. The partnership was formed in 1993 on the initiative of Charles Pollard, then chief constable of Thames Valley Police, as a forum in which chief officers of relevant criminal justice and local government services could share ideas and see if they could adopt a common approach to issues of community safety. It was a natural continuation of work I had begun in the Home

Office. The role was later taken by community safety and then Crime and Disorder Reduction Partnerships and by local criminal justice boards, and the partnership now brings together the resources of organizations in the statutory, private and voluntary sectors to develop schemes to help offenders and victims and their families, and others who are vulnerable or in difficulty. An important element is the contribution which can be made by the arts. Its role has sometimes been brokerage — bringing people together, stimulating ideas, finding solutions and helping others to put them into effect. Schemes once tried and tested have sometimes been absorbed into mainstream provision, and Circles of Support and Accountability[6] and Escaping Victimhood[7] which began in England as part of the Thames Valley Partnership (TVP) have now become established as separate charities. Responding to the changing environment in which voluntary organizations now have to operate, TVPs more recent work has focused more on service delivery, with current examples which include restorative justice, mentoring for prisoners in the critical period immediately after release, support for defendants' families at court and protection for victims of domestic violence. The partnership has evolved continuously to adjust itself to changes in its environment and sources of funding, and it has shown remarkable resilience and ingenuity in doing so. It is a creative organization, founded on a clear sense of values, and it is probably unique in this country[8].

The Situation Today

The changes in criminal justice, and in public services more generally, are taking place in a context of wider shifts in the character of British, and especially English, society. Britain is in many respects a more liberal society, and perhaps more 'free', than it was 50 years ago. Social distinctions are less prominent, and there are fewer prejudices and more tolerance in matters of personal behaviour and relationships. In many respects, and for many people, life is 'better' than it used to be. The last 30 years have however seen a changes in public attitudes and sensibilities which become more punitive,

---

6. Working to reduce sex offending — see www.circles-uk.org.uk
7. Supporting people whose lives have been disrupted by serious crime, especially murder and manslaughter — see www.escapingvictimhood.com
8. See www.thamesvalleypartnership.org.uk

and a shift in public values towards individualism, competitiveness and intolerance of failure. The changes are in attitudes not only towards crime and people who commit it, but also towards others who do not 'belong', for example because they are 'immigrants', or who are not 'deserving' because they 'live off the state'.

Governments' approaches to public policy have been increasingly dominated by neo-classical economic models, with their emphasis on rational choice, individual choice and material disincentives and rewards, and their assumption that human behaviour is in the end determined by material self-interest. Other social sciences and other explanations of human behaviour have been neglected.[9] The 'market' has become the model for the provision and governance of all public services. In criminal justice, protecting the public and reducing reoffending are proclaimed as objectives, but the means by which those ends are to be achieved are often based on dubious assumptions about effectiveness and 'what works'. They often involve bureaucratic and laborious processes of micromanagement and 'competing' and commissioning which affect government departments, operational services and voluntary organizations alike (see previous chapter). The new orthodoxy has become so pervasive that it is now hard to challenge its assumptions, and more difficult to 'speak truth to power'.

The term 'liberal' has come to be used as one of abuse, often without much thought for what it means. I have always understood it to mean a commitment to the values of freedom, democracy, social justice, respect for the individual and protection from oppression by corporate interests or the state. Critics now associate it with weakness, complacency and social irresponsibility and by doing so diminish the fundamental values for which it stands. Politicians and others praise the liberal values for which the country fought two world wars, but rarely apply them to contemporary situations.

Criminal justice has to cope with uncertainty and diversity; it has to recognise and respect the human emotions of anger and fear but also those of courage and hope. Its managers and practitioners have to engage with real lives as they are lived in the world and should not hide behind a screen of jargon, risk-assessment and performance management.

---

9.   See for example Paul Ormerod's *Positive Linking* (London: Faber and Faber, 2012) and his earlier *Why Most Things Fail* (Faber and Faber, 2005).

The relationship between government and the courts has become more complicated and in some respects more tense, especially with the growth of judicial review and the Human Rights Act 1998 as described in the previous chapter, and the increasing complexity of legislation, not least on sentencing. The courts have come under criticism, including from ministers, in a way that would not have been contemplated 30 years ago.

Public service and public administration have become more politicised. Many more issues turn on a decision by ministers, and ministers are keen to present themselves as energetic and decisive in many more areas of national life. Events and arguments have come to be reported not for their own significance but as a 'boost' or a 'set back' for a particular minister or other individual. The need for 'public confidence' may be used to justify action regardless of any empirical evidence of the need or consequences. Public misunderstandings about subjects such as crime, social benefits and immigration become accepted as a basis for populist policies, with no attempt to correct them.

Political parties which had their origin in the social and economic structures of the nineteenth and early twentieth centuries no longer have the clear identities which they once displayed or certainty about the values they represent. They have moved towards the centre ground, now called the 'centre-right' and 'centre-left', making their appeals to the country more on claims to competence in government than on any distinctive vision of the country's future. The 'culture of blame' has extended to politics, where the aim is more to find fault with the other side than to work towards a solution. The austerity which followed the financial crisis in 2008 did not lead to a reduction in the use of imprisonment, as seemed possible during the first months of the Coalition government, but to a more intensive programme of outsourcing to the private sector.

Despite the strength of the support for Margaret Thatcher and Tony Blair and the governments they led, governments, political parties and England as a whole have become less sure of themselves, of their place in the world, and of the kind of country they want England to be (apart from those who would like it to be as they imagine it was at some time in the past). Inconclusive arguments take place about English or British 'identity' or the kind of history that should be taught in schools. National institutions such as the National Health Service, state schools, and the Civil Service are regularly portrayed as 'failing'. Governments constantly demand 'change', sometimes as much for its own sake and for appearances as for any practical outcome it might produce. The Conservative party sees a future in which as much as possible of the apparatus of the state is transferred to the private sector and made subject to the discipline of competition and the 'market', but all political parties are struggling to find support and are afraid to act decisively in any direction.

The American writer Philip Bobbitt has described the situation in Great Britain and the United States as the creation of a 'market state', based on maximising opportunities and satisfying expectations and demands, which has displaced the 'nation state' on which liberal values depend.[10] Whereas the old nation state based its legitimacy on a promise to better the material well-being of the nation as a whole, the market state promises to use the mechanisms of the commercial market to maximise the opportunities of each individual citizen. An emphasis on the responsibility, and the reward and penalisation, of individuals is one aspect; outsourcing and commissioning services from the private sector and payment by results are another. Commenting on Bobbitt's book, David Blunkett as Home Secretary welcomed the market state as being more democratic than a state dominated by a metropolitan elite; the former Archbishop of Canterbury, Dr Rowan Williams, criticised it as lacking a sense of moral values. It is also an abdication of political leadership.

This is not a promising situation for a programme of liberal reform, whether in criminal justice or in wider aspects of social policy. It is however one in which it is more than ever necessary to reaffirm and hold on to the values of fairness and justice, and of humanity and compassion, and to ensure that public services and the institutions of state are working together to protect them.

Some Conclusions

In this and the final section of this chapter I will draw together some of the threads which have run through the 'story' as I have told it, identify some

10. Philip Bobbitt, *The Shield of Achilles: War, Peace and the Course of History*, London, Allen Lane, Penguin Press, 2002.

of the lessons which were or might have been learned, and suggest some conclusions which may be of some permanent relevance beyond the events and circumstances at any particular time. They are also discussed in *Where Next for Criminal Justice?*, especially in Chapter 9 'The Role of Government in Criminal Justice', and Chapter 10 'Policy, Politics and the Way Forward'.

The situations in which criminal justice operates are complex and the outcomes of any action by government are uncertain. Complexity, uncertainty and risk are part of life: they have to be managed and cannot be avoided. There will always be unexpected and sometimes shocking events. Government should not over-react to them or add to them by imposing unnecessarily restrictive or complicated measures and procedures of its own. Legislation and administrative procedures should be as simple and straightforward as possible: complexity leads to obscurity, anomalies and oversights, and potentially to embarrassment and disaster. Progress will often be made more successfully through local initiatives which are adapted to local circumstances and engage local communities than through centrally-designed schemes 'rolled out' on a national scale.

Government should not try to show that it always has a solution and always knows best. Most crime is local and should be dealt with as a local problem and as a responsibility of local services and communities. Government should not be too concerned about the detail or 'post code' differences and should beware of 'league tables' which can be misunderstood and manipulated. Ministers and officials should avoid wishful thinking and be realistic about what can be achieved and what people should be led to expect. To reorganize or legislate for effect, to send a message or to create an impression of activity may only lead to disillusion and do little to solve the substantive problem. Constant activity and 'tough' language, so far from reassuring the public, may simply reinforce and legitimate people's fears.

The criminal law sets the outer limits of what the country as a whole considers to be acceptable behaviour—as Mary Tuck once said[11] 'to mark the limits of tolerance of society at large'—and it must have authority and legitimacy if the state is to demand its acceptance. It should be engaged sparingly and respectfully. Its scope and reach should not extend further than is necessary for a civilised society, where conduct will for most purposes be

---

11. At the Ditchley conference described in *Chapter 9*.

better regulated by social standards, cultural norms and individual conscience. Administrative safeguards cannot be relied upon to prevent oppressive enforcement if the law is too widely drawn. The criminal law should not be misused to 'send a message' or for political advantage or operational convenience.

Scholars and penal reformers in many countries are now arguing for a new and more 'civilised'—or less divisive and exclusively punitive—approach to crime and the treatment of those who commit or suffer from it[12]. Their scheme would be based on restorative justice (see *Chapter 8*) and sometimes a 'middle' system of justice (see *Chapter 9*). The latter is beyond the horizon of any government or political party in this country at present, but restorative justice is attracting more political and professional interest than it has done in the past. It might in time transform criminal justice if there is the political will to take it seriously and it is treated as a vision and not just another process or a commodity to be traded in the market place.

Democracy is about more than elections, and the fact of having been elected to an office is not by itself enough to give authority or legitimacy to those in positions of power. It should be a continuous, transparent and inclusive process of listening and responding—and not doing so only to the loudest voices, which the print and social media can amplify so that they drown all others. While more issues have become politicised, fewer people feel that they can have an influence on them, and those who want to 'get things done' feel frustrated by the delays and compromises which democratic processes involve.[13] Democracy needs a public that is well-informed about the issues, including those such as crime, immigration, and social security where the facts are widely misrepresented and misunderstood. That in turn requires complete and accurate presentation by government, effective engagement by service providers with users and local communities, and honest and

---

12. See for example David Cornwell, John Blad and Martin Wright (eds.), *Civilising Criminal Justice: An International Restorative Agenda for Penal Reform*, Sherfield-on-Loddon: Waterside Press, 2013. The volume contains contributions from 12 different countries in Europe and the Commonwealth.

13. David Runciman has analysed that frustration in his book *The Confidence Trap: A History of Democracy in Crisis from World War I to the Present*, Princeton University Press, 2014.

proportionate reporting by the media[14]. Public servants themselves need to engage directly with the public in ways which generate and sustain mutual understanding and trust, especially if significant numbers or people lack confidence in a country's democratic institutions or do not take part in the democratic process.

The former Archbishop of Canterbury [Dr] Rowan Williams has argued that

> 'Good, "legitimate" government involves both direct election and mechanisms for representing
>
> (i) Concerns that are of longer-term importance than electoral cycles allow;
>
> (ii) Minority interests that can be silenced by large electoral majorities;
>
> (iii) Groups with conscientious reservations about aspects of public policy; and
>
> (iv) The expertise of professional and civil society agents that will not necessarily be engaged in party political elections.'[15]

Much of the evidence about crime and those who commit it is counter-intuitive and is not what people expect. Reassuring information, for example the fall in crime from the mid-1990s onwards, is often disbelieved. A large proportion of the male population has criminal convictions or admits to having committed criminal offences, and many victims of crime are or have been offenders, and *vice versa*. Whatever legitimate concern or sympathy there may be for victims of crime, it is misleading to talk of 'innocent victims' and the 'law-abiding majority', and invidious to contrast them with 'criminals' as if offenders were a separate class of people, or to present the interests of offenders and victims as if they were in some way opposed to one another. Government departments and services should actively present and explain the facts, and challenge attempts to misrepresent them. Public understanding is a necessary condition for public confidence.

---

14. In his book *Democracy Under Attack: How the Media Distort Policy and Politics* (Bristol: The Policy Press, 2012) Malcolm Dean has described how democracy can be undermined by the choice of events or facts that are to be reported, by the emphasis given to one subject or aspect of a story rather than another, or by a concentration on personalities and disputes rather than policies or issues.

15. Rowan Williams 'Sovereignty, Democracy, Justice: Elements of a Good Society', Eighth lecture in the Magna Carta Lecture Series, hosted by Royal Holloway, University of London and run in association with the Magna Carta Trust. *Justice Reflections*, Issue 35, No. 237, 2014, 1.

Language matters. Governments should avoid using the images and terminology of exclusion, confrontation and especially warfare, with their implication that some people are of less value, or do not 'belong', because of who they are or the situation in which they are placed. Language should not be 'loaded' to score political points. Obscure expressions, jargon and clichés can give the impression of an arcane institution from which outsiders are excluded. Governments should use simple language which shows that they respect their audience and not 'talk down' either to the public or to public servants. George Orwell has warned of the danger of 'Newspeak', where the exceptional is made to seem commonplace and what is threatening is made to appear reassuring, and of 'doublethink' by which people can be persuaded to accept wholly unrealistic expectations.

Government should maintain a continuous, open and respectful process of discussion with the various components of the criminal justice system and with those who are affected by it, including interest groups and academics. Contact should not be confined to formal processes of consultation. Everyone with an interest should understand what is happening and why; they should feel able to contribute, and that they have been heard even if the outcome is not the one they would have liked. The questions asked should not close off options or areas for discussion. The aim should be to achieve a sense of shared ownership of what is to be done and a shared commitment to its success. People should do things because they believe in them, not just because it is what they have been told to do.

The Civil Service has never had, and should not have, a monopoly of advice to ministers. Earlier chapters have referred to the advice which came from Royal Commissions and other advisory bodies, including the Advisory Council on the Penal System. There is no reason why advice should not come from other sources provided that they are openly acknowledged and the advice is accessible to public scrutiny, but those sources must be clearly distinguished from organizations or individuals with a commercial interest in the outcome or pressure groups that represent a particular point of view.

Civil servants should have a 'hinterland', an understanding of the world in which their department operates, a collective memory, and the professional knowledge to make sure that their judgement is sound and their actions and advice are realistic. They should try to help ministers and their political advisers to share that understanding and not become isolated in their own political world. Most issues have arisen before and have been dealt with in the past. Government should not neglect the lessons of history, and should value and encourage a departmental memory. Departments need an identity and continuity; they are not the minister's private estate.

Relationships and dynamics will in the end count for more than reforms of structures and legislation. Reform may sometimes be needed, but it will be at the price of distraction and disruption and the new arrangements will only be as good as the improvement in relationships and dynamics that they make possible. The culture should be one of continuous improvement, of doing things better, and not one of constant change which too easily becomes one of change for its own sake. Visible success is more likely to be found in what people experience for themselves than in statistics or tick-boxes — they see that things work well, what is supposed to happen does happen, they feel they are treated properly and know what to expect and where they stand. They should be thought of and respected as people, and not as an assembly of 'needs' and 'risks' which have to be 'addressed' as if the person was a machine to be serviced.

Final Thoughts

The view which the Home Office took of its functions and responsibilities at the end of the 1950s, described in *Chapter 1*, was still more or less in place at the beginning of the 1990s, although Charles Cunningham's language might by then have seemed rather quaint and there would have been more emphasis on accountability and on equality in respect of race, gender and religion. We had become more hesitant about proclaiming departmental values as such, especially in abstract terms, and it was easier to say 'what we do', as in the mission statement for the Prison Service (see *Chapter 4*)[16] As I saw them, they were the Rule of Law, the independence of the judiciary, protection of human rights and proportionality of response; together with basic principles of tolerance, good faith, procedural fairness, and a respect for individuals which recognises both the principle of equality before the

---

16. In 2006 the government defined the Department's values as 'We deliver for the public; we are professional and innovative; we work openly and collaboratively; we treat everyone with respect'.

law and their equal value as citizens and human beings. They included humanity and compassion. They were set alongside the Civil Service values of integrity, honesty, objectivity and impartiality which are now set out in the Civil Service Code. I thought of those values as the foundation on which the professionalism of the Civil Service is based, and as providing the department's 'moral compass', even though it did not always live up to them in practice.

Those values were already being overlaid by the changes in public attitudes and sensibilities mentioned earlier in this chapter, and the changes have become more pronounced since that time. In a democracy, government departments and public services have to move with the spirit of the times, but I hope those values would still be recognised and respected in the Home Office, the Ministry of Justice and other government departments today, even if their interpretation and application have changed in some respects. I have asked myself many times whether they belong to an era which has now passed, but I cannot persuade myself that they are no longer relevant. To argue for them is not to try to return to the past, but to find a sense of direction for the future.[17]

---

17. This chapter was in preparation when the Department of Health published *Improving the Safety of Patients in England,* a report from the National Advisory Group on the Safety of Patients in England chaired by Dr Don Berwick. Its conclusions included '…the system must

- Recognise with clarity and courage the need for wide system change.
- Abandon blame as a tool and trust the goodwill and good intentions of the staff.
- Use quantitative targets with caution. Such goals do have an important role *en route* to progress, but should never displace the primary goal of better care.
- Recognise that transparency is essential and expect and insist on it.
- Ensure that responsibility for functions related to safety and improvement are vested clearly and simply
- Give the people of the NHS career-long help to learn, master and apply modern methods for quality control, quality improvement and quality planning.
- Make sure pride and joy in work, not fear, infuse the NHS.
  Substituting 'justice' for 'care', the same conclusions would apply to criminal justice.

Transforming the Home Office — I

David Faulkner[1]
University of Oxford Centre for Criminology

1. This is the first of two papers which respond to the Home Secretary's letter of 19th July in which he asked for comments on the documents published at the same time to 'place Public Protection at the heart of we do'. This paper is concerned principally with the character and culture of the Home Office itself; the second deals with criminal justice and penal policy.

2. The Capability Review has rightly recognised the need for the Home Office to have a clear vision and sense of direction. The Home Office has sometimes given the impression that it is driven almost entirely by a political need to react to events and to promote short term initiatives, without much regard for any longer term sense of coherence or even purpose. It has resembled a vehicle being driven at high speed, but without adequate brakes or steering.

3. Statements of values and strategic priorities are among the means which are necessary to sustain that vision and sense of direction. They need to be periodically refreshed and kept up to date,[2] and they have to be applied in complex, changing and often politically charged situations. The 'values' as now set out[3] are more a description of 'how we work' than a statement of values as such. The values which guide the Department include, for example, the Rule of Law,

---

1. 'Transforming the Home Office I and II', *Prison Service Journal*, 171, 17-23, 2007, reproduced by kind permission.
2. There was a similar exercise, in different circumstances and with a lower profile, in 1991. One outcome was the two papers *Management of Change: Whitehall Experience* by Sir Clive Whitmore, and *Continuity and Change in the Home Office* by David Faulkner (see page 146 and 160).
3. 'We deliver for the public
   we are professional and innovative
   we work openly and collaboratively
   we treat everyone with respect'.

the independence of the judiciary, protection of human rights, proportion-ality of response, and basic principles such as tolerance, good faith, procedural fairness and respect for individuals which recognises both the principle of equality before the law and their equal value as citizens and human beings.

4. Those values are sometimes seen as part of the British 'national identity' and they transcend party politics. They are not unique to Great Britain and certainly not to the Home Office, and they apply to government and public service in most democratic countries. They are reflected in various interna-tional instruments. They have provided the Department's 'moral compass', probably for most of its history, although it may not always have lived up to them in practice. If 're-balancing', and the current criticism of liberal values more generally, imply that they are not longer suitable for the modern world, that needs to be stated and argued. If not, they should be recognised, respected and 'owned' by the Department as a whole.

5. Language is important, not only politically to gain public support but also to communicate effectively with staff, partners and so-called stakeholders. The language in which government conducts its business is often criticised for its obscurity and its sometimes aggressive use of jargon and clichés. That criticism needs to be taken seriously in situations where partnerships and mutual understanding and confidence are becoming increasingly important. An equally serious concern is that government regularly uses the images and terminology of confrontation and warfare, with 'criminals' as an implied enemy who is of less value than the 'law-abiding' and 'hard-working' citizens and from whom they need to be protected. That is a false distinction, and the analogy of warfare is misleading. 'Victory' is never possible, impressions of failure lead to disillusion and undermine confidence. Such language can also been heard as an encouragement or justification of abuses of power and due process. Its effect can be to deepen the social divisions and increase the anxiety which the Government itself wishes to prevent. It should have no place in white papers or other considered statements of government policy or in official press releases.[4] Nor is it necessary for government to 'talk down' to public services in its circulars and notices, as often happens at present.

---

4.   The white paper *Justice for All*, CM5563, London: TSO, 2002, was a particularly bad example.

6. 'Protecting the public' obviously is and always has been a central task of the Home Office. It resembles the function which used to be called 'keeping the Queen's Peace', although without the same overtones of legitimacy and due process. In present circumstances, the Home Office must inevitably focus even more narrowly on public protection and the associated issues of risk and security. With the transfer of so many of its functions to other departments, public protection can reasonably be said to have become the Department's 'core purpose'. But a single-minded concentration on public protection will still leave unresolved tensions between that and the wider issues of race and religion, and of justice and human rights. It may be a more healthy situation for those tensions to be resolved across rather than within departments, but it will be important to ensure that the wider issues are thoroughly understood in the Department for Communities and Local Government and the Department for Constitutional Affairs respectively, and that all three Departments are fully committed to sustaining the underlying principles. The DCA should now be regarded more formally as a 'department of justice', with responsibilities which should include not only human rights but also, in due course, sentencing.

7. The Capability Review states, correctly, that 'The culture within the Senior Civil Service also needs to place greater value on the corporate responsibility for talent management, and staff development and redeployment.' That responsibility has arguably been neglected in recent years, as staff have increasingly been expected to plan their own careers and more posts have been filled by open or internal competition. But talent has to be 'grown' as well as 'managed', and so do expertise and the much neglected quality of wisdom. The responsibility identified in the Review should extend to those qualities as well. The Home Office should give serious attention to the way in which it is discharged, and the respect which is accorded to those qualities in practice. The point will be particularly relevant in connection with 'contestability', or 'public value partnerships', where alternative providers may prefer to buy in talent and expertise from the public sector rather than develop it themselves. Similar arguments apply to the use of consultants.

8. The Home Office should take seriously the need, which the Review says it recognises, to 'strengthen the information, analysis and evidence used in the formulation of strategies' and to 'work more collaboratively with partners and stakeholders'. The impression from outside the Department is that a fundamental change is needed in the culture which seems to have been developed in recent years, where performance and delivery have been pursued without enough regard to evidence or genuine consultation, often under pressure from ministers for new initiatives and 'quick wins'. That is in spite of the emphasis on 'what works', and of numerous exercises in consultation, where the purpose has seemed to be more to seek support for what has already been decided than draw in new information or ideas or generate any sense of shared ownership. Perhaps because of the Department's now overwhelmingly political agenda, the relationship between the Home Office and its 'delivery agents and partners' has too often been one-sided and each has too often regarded the other more as an obstacle to be avoided or overcome than as a genuine partner in a shared enterprise. 'A sense of shared ownership and strategy' has to be made a reality, and serious thought should be given to the means by which it is to be achieved. They should include mechanisms of local accountability, to which the Government as a whole now seems to be paying increasing attention.

9. For the Review still to criticise a 'lack of strategic coherence or integrated working' suggests that little progress can have been made since 'interdependence' and 'managing the system as a whole' first started to receive serious attention 25 years ago. The lack of progress may have been an unintended consequence of the political priorities which ministers pursued during the intervening period; and of the 'sharp personal focus on PSA targets', and on performance indicators more generally, which can too easily generate a defensive attitude and a 'silo mentality'.

10. The Reform Action Plan reproduces some of the same material, and includes a reference to new 'contract' between ministers and officials, 'clarifying respective roles and expectations in relation policy, operational delivery and management'. The nature, status and content of the 'contract', and the

methods by which it is monitored and enforced, will be matters of considerable interest and importance.

11. The distinction between 'policy', which is for ministers, and 'delivery' which is for civil servants, is often convenient. But it is difficult to sustain in practice. Civil servants are still responsible for the quality of the advice they give at the stage when the policy is being formulated, and should also guide the process of research, consultation and analysis by which the policy should be informed. Ministers are entitled not to take the advice that is offered; to take advice from elsewhere; or to decide that no advice, research or consultation is needed and they can rely on their own political judgement. Or they may select, or intimidate, their advisers so that the only advice they receive is what it is politically convenient to hear. Whatever the situation, the process should be transparent and the considerations and the influences should be capable of being made known and assessed, after a suitable interval if not immediately. Civil servants and ministers should both take responsibility for what may then be found.

12. Notions of Ministerial and Civil Service accountability have shifted over the years. It has become accepted that officials and not ministers should take responsibility for actions or situations of which ministers had no knowledge and which they did not intend. Even so, the increasing politicisation of public business, and ministers' increasing involvement in the management of their departments, make the distinction harder to sustain and individual responsibility harder to assign. Recent experience in the Home Office, and possibly in other departments concerned with social policy, suggests that civil servants' accountability to ministers needs a better understanding, by all concerned, of the dynamics and relationships involved in managing public business; a greater degree of mutual confidence and trust; and more respect for continuity, skills, experience and the wisdom mentioned above.

13. Civil and some other public servants have changed their focus from 'serving the country', or 'serving the public', to 'serving ministers'. A generation ago, civil servants and ministers both saw themselves as having a common but independent duty to serve the public or the national interest,

or sometimes 'the Crown' as a symbol of the national interest. The culture seems now to be one of exclusive service and accountability to ministers, and of largely unquestioning compliance with ministers' wishes and suspension of independent judgement. With that change, and perhaps reflecting the attitudes and style of successive governments, has come a culture of blame and risk-avoidance, of 'playing safe' and 'protecting one's back'. Civil servants have seemed reluctant, or sometimes unable, to point out difficulties for fear of being thought obstructive or not sufficiently committed. They have become more cautious in what they think they can say, in private as well as in public. Pressures in the office, often from ministers themselves, make it hard for them to go out 'onto the street' or to engage in a genuine meeting of minds. They are often poorly equipped to anticipate the practical effect of new rules and procedures when they are applied on the ground, or to appreciate that effect when the new rules have come into operation.

14. Civil servants' accountability should not only be a matter of relationships and communications upwards to senior managers and ministers, and of compliance with instructions or controls that are passed downwards. It should also include their lateral relationships with colleagues, 'stakeholders' and the public. Another consequence of the 'performance culture' is that civil and other public servants have over the last ten or fifteen years become more narrowly focused on their 'upward' rather than their 'outward' relationships, both within and outside government. The 'silo' mentality has persisted and even been re-enforced, despite efforts to overcome it.

15. The Government should consider the kind of institutional framework that is now needed to support and sustain its programme of progressive reform. Examples could include an institute or centre for criminal justice to promote and protect standards and commission research, perhaps resembling the National Institute for Clinical Excellence; a college for professional training and development; and the encouragement (though not direct provision) of spaces where practitioners, academics and policy makers and judges can meet an exchange ideas on equal terms and in a 'safe' environment.

26th September, 2006

Transforming the Home Office — II

David Faulkner
University of Oxford Centre for Criminology

1. This is the second of two papers which respond to the Home Secretary's request, in his letter of 19th July, for comments on the documents published at that time to 'place Public Protection at the heart of what we do'. The first was concerned principally with the character and culture of the Home Office itself; this paper deals with criminal justice and penal policy.

2. The situation remains precarious and the prospects are still uncertain. Many of the Government's policies have implied, and continue to imply, greater use of imprisonment, for longer periods, and more intensive supervision in the community, for which insufficient provision had been made. The extra provision now planned may not be adequate, or it may be too late.

3. The evidence for 'what works' is still dubious. Evaluations have shown that some programmes or interventions can help, for the right people and in the right circumstances, but the emphasis is too often on 'outputs' (how many offenders have been put through the programme), and not enough on 'outcomes' (what difference has it made). In setting national targets for reducing rates of re-conviction, government risks raising unrealistic expectations of what the criminal justice system can deliver. The methodological difficulties of demonstrating connections between cause and effect are well known. Now that criminal justice has become so politicised, any claims based on statistics or research are likely to be met by scepticism or disbelief. Failure, or a perception of failure, is likely to be exploited by the media to create a public and ultimately political reaction which is disproportionate and badly informed. The proposals announced in July can be supported or

criticised on their individual merits, but they are unlikely to have more than a marginal or to the public imperceptible effect on crime.

4. History is more likely to judge the National Offender Management Service not so much on the statistics of reconviction as on the extent to which the system 'works' — in the sense that what is supposed to happen does happen, at the right time, in the right place and for the right people; that offenders complete programmes and comply with orders and conditions; and that courts, other services and voluntary organisations are able to rely on NOMS to work with them in a spirit genuine co-operation and understanding, and on equal and mutually agreed terms. Staff, offenders, their families and victims need to know that they will be properly treated, where they stand and what they can expect. As has repeatedly been shown, those things do not always happen at present, for various reasons which include pressures on resources and prison overcrowding, but sometimes also the unintended — but often foreseeable — effects of the Government's own actions.

5. Risk assessment can be valuable for deciding what kind of programme, treatment or intervention an offender might need or benefit from. But it is never more than a judgement of probabilities. It creates situations where any likelihood of risk has to be matched by measures to meet the risk, even though it may be quite remote, sometimes at considerable cost to the system and to the offender. The validity and legitimacy of risk assessment are especially questionable when it is used to decide the length of an offender's sentence or date of release — in effect the severity of a person's punishment.[1] It is positively dangerous when false claims are made for its scientific accuracy[2], so that any subsequent offence is seen as a professional or operational failure which calls for what may be disproportionate action to prevent any

---

1. Recent legislation and policy have confused the nature, purpose and legitimacy of punishment as it is administered by the state. For a more extended discussion, see 'Prospects for Progress in Penal Practice', forthcoming in *Criminology and Criminal Justice*, 7/2, 135-152 (2007).
2. The belief in what has become in effect a 'science of interventions' resembles in some ways the belief that science could transform society and solve the problem of crime that was current for a time in the 1960s. The resulting disillusion affected criminal justice thinking for most of a generation.

repetition. The difficulty of judging risk and then of acting on the judgement is only too familiar to the police

6. The mechanisms of 'contestability', or 'public value partnerships', can be used in different ways, with different underlying objectives. It is not yet clear how the Government, or Regional Offender Managers, intend that they should be used in practice. They can be used competitively, to save costs, impose standardisation and uniformity, and punish or threaten punishment for failure. Or they can be used co-operatively to encourage innovation and experiment. They can be rigid and 'top-down', requiring compliance with a centrally-imposed specification, or they can be flexible and help to promote local creativity. The process can be complex, time-consuming and bureaucratic, encouraging artificial devices to gain favour or win contracts, or it can be open and accessible to new ideas from old or new sources. Commissioners can concentrate on getting best value from whatever competing sources are already available, or they can accept a public responsibility to use the process of commissioning in ways which will 'grow' the skills and capacity, and the values and relationships, that will be needed for the future. The process will be particularly difficult for voluntary organisations, especially smaller or local organisations which may have most to offer in terms of innovation and 'making a difference'. The outcomes of commissioning could be beneficial or disastrous, depending on the choices that are made.

7. More effective management of offenders was arguably the most important justification for the creation of NOMS, and it is the most promising feature of the reform. It is not yet clear how offender managers will be organized or enabled to do the work; what authority they will have to give directions to service providers or to commission facilities; what co-operation they can expect from agencies or communities outside the criminal justice system; what standing and authority they will have in the courts, among colleagues in other criminal justice services or in local communities; or what accountability they will have towards or from them. Nor is it clear how far they will be able to form any continuing and consistent relationship with offenders or their families, or to promote supportive relationships with others who may have an influence on their lives. Recent research has demonstrated that any

effect on rates of re-offending will depend crucially on how such relationships can be formed and sustained.

8. Any progress will be difficult while capacity and demand are so far out of alignment. The Government has made promises and raised expectations that may prove to have too weak a foundation to sustain them. Their foundation needs to be strengthened and broadened. That could be done by developing or introducing policies or practices on the following lines.

(a) Greater emphasis on the responsibilities of citizens and civil society, and on the relationships and structures through which those responsibilities can be exercised more effectively and with more accountability.

(b) A stronger focus on repairing damage, putting things right, restoring and building relationships, taking responsibility, to be done by everyone — offenders, staff, other services, communities — sometimes as part of a punishment, sometimes not.

(c) Acknowledging the limitations of the criminal justice process as an instrument of social engineering or crime control, and where possible resolving situations by restorative, social or administrative measures, without recourse to the formal criminal justice process.

(d) Recognising that where conviction and punishment are still necessary, they should be used in accordance with the principles of proportionality and due process.

(e) Using criminal sanctions, when they have to be used and so far as possible, for a restorative or reparative purpose, for which the court, NOMS, the offender, communities and sometimes the victim should all take some responsibility.

9. More specific policies, or 'workstreams', might then focus on

Designing local structures and developing relationships to provide a stronger sense of local accountability, ownership and responsibility, taking into account the community justice centre and the community justice initiative which the Department for Constitutional Affairs is developing in Liverpool and Salford, and the proposals for re-organising the police.

(a) Within those structures, mechanisms for the review and resolution of local issues and situations, where possible without recourse to criminal proceedings or an adversarial criminal trial—especially for children.

(b) A closer relationship between sentencing and the administration of the sentence, and between sentencers, the services and offenders themselves, with a shared sense of accountability and responsibility for what the sentence can be expected to achieve and the demands it will make.

(c) Programmes and regimes which treat offenders as people and citizens, as having lives and responsibilities of their own, and not as objects or units in a system in which their identity is defined only by their criminality. For prison officers always to call prisoners by their names, and for prisoners to have the right to vote in Parliamentary elections, would be two symbolic examples.

(d) Programmes, structures and relationships to improve offenders' education, health, accommodation and employment so that they can be more self-reliant, responsible and productive members of society and less dependent on state benefits—building on the Green Paper *Reducing Re-Offending Through Skills and Employment* (CM 6702. London: TSO, 2005).

(e) An ambition for the longer term should be a new criminal code, for which the Law Commission and others have argued for a long time, designed to simplify the structure and with it the process of sentencing; to reduce the number of criminal offences and the scope of the criminal law; and to reverse the expansion which has taken place over the last ten years.

10. Difficult subjects will still include

(a) The treatment of risk and 'dangerousness', and how the public can best be protected from people who may be dangerous but who cannot be treated for mental illness without an abuse of punishment or human rights. Protection is needed, but indeterminate and extended sentences and refusal of parole—in effect, extra punishment—risk serious injustice. Problems of consistency, proportionality and disproportionate commitment of resources are already beginning to emerge from the special sentences for public protection that were introduced by the Criminal Justice Act, 2003.

(b) The need to establish a recognised boundary between those powers and functions which can properly be exercised only by a public authority on behalf of the state, within a framework of public accountability, and those which can be exercised by independent charitable or commercial providers if they able to provide a better or unique service.

(c) The contribution which should be expected from the academic community. Questions include the implications for criminology of the change in focus described in this paper; the kind of empirical or theoretical research that is needed to judge the effects or viability of the approaches it has suggested, and to provide a normative foundation on which its legitimacy as well as its public appeal might be based; the structures through which such research should be funded and commissioned; and how policy and academic work could be brought closer together.

11. The approach suggested in this paper is broadly consistent with, though it goes beyond, the Government's existing Strategy. ministers will obviously wish to avoid anything that which could be represented — or misrepresented — as 'soft on crime'. But it is consistent with several themes in the present Government's policy and speeches by ministers — on civil renewal; on 'respect'; on local responsibility and empowerment; and on a sense of national identity based on 'liberty, responsibility and fairness'. It could be seen as an extension and consolidation of existing policy, and a natural development of existing operational practice, not as a 'U turn' or a change of mind. It is at least as likely to 'work' in terms of reducing re-offending as the existing programmes and interventions. It is more likely to create the capacity, and the will, to change among offenders, and to generate confidence among the staff and ultimately among the wider public.

12. A question that is rarely asked in political, professional or academic debate is whether criminal justice, or modern society more generally, has any place for qualities such as compassion and forgiveness. There is none in the Government's policy as it is formulated at present, and where they do have a place, for example in restorative justice or Circles of Support and Accountability, they are sustained almost entirely by volunteers and voluntary organisations, often from a Christian background. Their only interest

to Government is in whether they can be shown to 'work' in reducing re-offending or increasing public confidence. All those affected by crime or involved in criminal justice, in whatever capacity, need some sense of hope and belief in the possibility of progress.

26th September, 2006

Index